THE ACHIEVEMENT OF JOHN HENRY NEWMAN

THE ACHIEVEMENT OF
JOHN HENRY NEWMAN

Ian Ker

COLLINS

First published in hardback in Great Britain in 1990
by HarperCollins*Religious* part of HarperCollins*Publishers* 77-85 Fulham Palace Road, London W6 8JB

First paperback printing 1991
Copyright © 1991 University of Notre Dame Press

Manufactured in the U.S.A.

ISBN 0 00599276 1

FOR MY PARENTS

CONTENTS

PREFACE

THIS BOOK IS NOT INTENDED to be a comprehensive survey of Newman's achievements as a thinker and writer. Thus, I have not discussed his poetry or his historical or political writings, to mention three obvious examples. Rather, I have deliberately concentrated on those aspects of Newman's achievement which seem to me to constitute his essential genius.

Inevitably, the longest chapter is on the theologian, and this is, not unexpectedly, the area of Newman's writings which has been most explored. By contrast, Newman's literary achievement is still not only underrated but also to a considerable extent unperceived. The philosophical writings, which have generally been highly regarded as a contribution to Christian apologetics, have in recent decades received serious and sustained attention from philosophers of religion, but their wider philosophical significance has still not been sufficiently appreciated. In spite of the legendary fame of Newman's preaching in his own day, remarkably little has been written on either the homiletic or the literary quality of the sermons, although their spirituality and theology have been perceptively studied, not least by the founder of modern Newman studies, Charles Stephen Dessain (1907–76). Finally, while *The Idea of a University* has always been highly valued both as a stylistic masterpiece and as the classic statement of the ideal of liberal education, it seems that the main thrust of Newman's thought on education has been surprisingly misunderstood and even ignored.

It is, then, to these five central areas of Newman's works that this book is addressed. And as such it is perhaps unique among the many studies of Newman. Unlike previous books which tend to be either biographical or general or of a specialized nature, the present study attempts to consider Newman's achievement as a whole but in a focused and selective way. The centennial of his death in 1890 seems an appropriate time for such a critical reevaluation.

I am grateful to Don Briel and James Reidy, colleagues at the College of St. Thomas, who encouraged me by their helpful comments and criticism, to complete this book; to Mrs. Virginia Lyons who once again transformed a primitive, handwritten manuscript into a modern typescript; to Ann Rice, my editor, who saved me from a number of slips and solecisms.

St. Paul, Minnesota
May 1989   I.T.K.

1

THE EDUCATOR

LIKE NEARLY ALL NEWMAN'S books, *The Idea of a University* (1873) is an "occasional" work. The first half consists of the *Discourses on the Scope and Nature of University Education* (1852), the lectures Newman was commissioned to deliver as a prelude to launching the new Catholic University of Ireland. The second half, which is much less well-known (indeed, in talking about the *Idea of a University*, people often mean simply the *Discourses*), consists of a fairly miscellaneous collection of talks and articles which Newman wrote as Rector of the university. In fact, the *Lectures and Essays* (1859) are generally more practical and usefully complement the more theoretical *Discourses*. Although it is the one recognized educational classic that exists, the *Idea* is very far from being a systematic treatise on education.

Running through the work is a preoccupation with religion and theology which many will find distracting, if not worse. This is partly due to the intensely personal character of Newman's writings, where he allows his own concerns and interests the freest possible play; but to a far greater extent it is the result of the "occasional" nature of the book itself. Newman had been asked originally to give some lectures in Dublin to persuade Irish Catholics of the importance of a *Catholic* university education. He was not altogether happy with the specific brief, if only because Irish Catholics were already deeply divided on the practicality and even desirability of having a

1

Catholic university at all. He also had to contend with the hostility of Irish nationalists to the prospect of the university being headed by an Englishman. The need to conciliate and reconcile these different points of view is at the heart of the rhetorical art of the first *Discourses,* where Newman attempts to promote the idea of a university which will be both Catholic and Irish and also a real university, as opposed to a clerical seminary.[1]

Not only are the *Discourses* as a whole a work of great rhetorical skill, but the whole book is a triumph of literary art, perhaps the finest extended example of nonfictional prose in the English language. Newman himself at the time called the *Discourses* one of his "two most perfect works, artistically."[2] Certainly nowhere else, except in the last great chapter of the *Apologia,* does Newman's rhetoric achieve more powerful and more subtle expression. As a strictly literary work, *The Idea of a University* will be considered later in this study.[3]

My purpose, however, in this chapter is to look at the *Idea* as an educational work, what Newman himself came in the end to regard as one of the five "constructive" books he had written.[4] This means detaching and isolating some central educational themes from both the particular Irish context and from Newman's own religious and theological preoccupations.

It is hardly necessary to apologize for this approach. After all, Newman himself wrote in 1863, "from first to last, education . . . has been my line."[5] His career at Oxford had begun with his election in 1822 to a fellowship at Oriel College, "at that time the object of ambition of all rising men in Oxford."[6] After that he "never wished any thing better or higher than . . . 'to live and die a fellow of Oriel.'"[7] In fact, the Tractarian Movement might never have begun but for Newman's quarrel with the Provost of Oriel over the role of a college tutor, Newman wanting a more direct, personal teaching relationship with undergraduates. As a result of being deprived of his tutorship, his teaching career at Oxford—in which his "heart was wrapped up"[8]—came to an end, and he turned to research into the Fathers and the history of the early Church. After becoming a Catholic, he was opposed to the restoration of the English hierarchy on the ground that "we want seminaries far more than sees. We want education."[9] So when the chance came of helping to found the new university in Dublin, Newman jumped at it, since he had "from the very first month of my Catholic existence . . . wished for a Catholic University."[10] Later, he was naturally attracted by the idea of founding the Oratory School; as an educational work, it fell "under those objects, to which I have especially given my time and thought."[11] And as an old man of sixty-three, he so enjoyed filling in for an absent teacher that he declared that "if I could believe it to be God's will, [I] would turn away my thoughts from ever writing any thing, and should see, in the superintendence of these boys, the nearest return to my Oxford life."[12] He was proud to claim that the school had "led the way in a system of educational improvement on a large scale through the Catholic community."[13] There is no doubt that in a very real sense Newman felt called to be an educator and teacher, even if his life turned out rather differently.

One obvious difficulty that faces the modern reader of the *Idea* is its strong element of hyperbole. The kind of rhetorical exaggeration that came naturally to the Victorians is unpalatable in a culture which tends to laud realism and deprecate idealism. The hyperbolism, therefore, which characterizes the *Idea of a University* is calculated to confuse and mislead the contemporary reader who takes literally what Newman and the readers of his time would have seen as a kind of exaggerated "approximation" to the truth.

Take, for example, Newman's concept of what he calls "special Philosophy" or "Liberal or Philosophical Knowledge," which he sees as "the end of University Education" and which he defines as "a comprehensive view of truth in all its branches, of the relations of science to science, of their mutual bearings, and their respective values."[14] Such high-sounding language has, perhaps not unnaturally, seriously misled at least two contemporary commentators. Thus, one of them wonders whether it is "the province of special courses in logic and metaphysics."[15] Another opines that it is "not the same as all the sciences taken together but . . . a science distinct from them and yet in some sense embodying the materials of them all," a "discipline" in fact with "a rather mysterious character."[16] But in reality Newman's "philosophy of an imperial intellect," as he elsewhere terms it, again somewhat hyperbolically, is not, as one might expect, some "superscience" or master "mode of knowing."[17] What Newman has in mind is something much more prosaic and simple. Rhetorical hyperbolism has led him to expand somewhat on that "real cultivation of mind" which he explained in the Preface to the *Discourses* as "the intellect . . . properly trained and formed to have a connected view or grasp of things."[18] This is shown by his definition of *Philosophy*—"In default of a recognized term, I have called the perfection or virtue of the intellect by the name of philosophy, philosophical knowledge, enlargement of mind, or illumination"[19]—by which he does not mean the academic subject called philosophy but "Knowledge . . . when it is acted upon, informed . . . impregnated by Reason," in other words knowledge which "grasps what it perceives through the senses . . . which takes a view of things; which sees more than the senses convey; which reasons upon what it sees, and while it sees; which invests it with an idea." And Newman implicitly recognizes his inclination to hyperbole when he remarks, "to have mapped out the Universe is the boast, or at least the ambition, of Philosophy."[20] Misunderstanding of Newman on this point is hardly conducive to appreciating the principle which is the heart and soul of his educational philosophy—what indeed one of the two commentators referred to rightly calls "the ability to think."[21]

All too often it is assumed that Newman's advocacy of education meant that he wanted people to study the liberal arts for the kind of reasons that it is conventionally argued they should be studied. If so, it is remarkable that in his several discussions of literature, for example, he does not emphasize its humanizing effect. It is true that he acknowledges that literature is the "history" of man, "his Life and Remains," "the manifestation of human nature in human language." And he points out that if "the power of speech is a gift as great as any that can be named . . . it will not answer to make light of Literature or to neglect its study."[22] But there is no attempt to claim that the study of literature has a peculiarly civilizing effect on our sensibility, for example, or even that a knowledge of certain literary authors is essential for one to be "educated." In "Christianity and Letters" he points out that traditionally "the Classics, and the subjects of thought and the studies to which they give rise, or . . . the Arts, have ever, on the whole, been the instruments of education"; these liberal arts were able in the middle ages to withstand the challenge of the new sciences of Scholastic theology, law, and medicine, because they were "acknowledged, as before, to be the best instruments of mental cultivation, and the best guarantees for intellectual progress." This for Newman is the "simple" test: "how best to strengthen, refine, and enrich the intellectual powers." And what seems to him self-evident is that "the perusal of the poets, historians, and philosophers of Greece and Rome will accomplish this purpose, as long experience has shown." Now that the liberal arts are again threatened, this time by the rise of the experimental sciences, the same question arises as before: will these sciences be able to train the mind as well as the humanities? Newman merely observes that it "is proved to us as yet by no experience whatever"; but again he insists: "the question is not what department of study contains the more wonderful facts, or promises the more brilliant discoveries, and which is in the higher and which in an inferior rank; but simply which out of all provides the most robust and invigorating discipline for the unformed mind."[23]

Newman could hardly have put the point more plainly: it is not an education in the liberal arts as such which makes a liberal education; rather it is the "discipline" and the "mental cultivation" traditionally held to result from the study of the liberal arts which makes a liberal education. From this point of view Newman thought that even theology, far more important for him as a branch of knowledge, was inferior educationally. If it could be shown that a scientific or theological course of studies could train the mind as effectively, then the study would be considered by Newman to provide an equally "liberal" education. Whatever the value inherent in the subject matter of studying arts subjects, that is not Newman's central concern: it is not "culture" in the modern sense of the word that he is concerned with, but "mental cultivation," that is, the training of the mind. Newman's understanding of a liberal education, then, is much more narrowly and specifically intellectual than that of the conventional advocate of an arts education.

In the Preface to the *Discourses* he states his case in the simplest terms and all interpretations of the *Discourses* should be compared with and tested against this basic statement of the thesis to ensure that hyperbole has not obscured the issue. There "real cultivation of mind" is deemed to be "the force, the steadiness, the comprehensiveness and the versatility of intellect, the command over our own powers, the instinctive just estimate of things as they pass before us." Newman appeals to our ordinary experience of life, not to draw our attention to the lack of "culture" or knowledge in people generally, but rather to the fact that so many people in everyday conversation are illogical, inconsistent, "never see the point," "are hopelessly obstinate and prejudiced." He is not, in the first place, desiderating people who appreciate classical music or painting or literature, let alone people who have achieved a high degree of knowledge. The object of a university education is to produce thinking people, no more and no less.

When the intellect has once been properly trained and formed to have a connected view or grasp of things, it will display its powers with more or less effect according to its particular quality and capacity in the individual. In the case of most men it makes itself felt in the good sense, sobriety of thought, reasonableness, candour, self-command, and steadiness of view, which charac-

terize it. . . . In all it will be a faculty of entering with comparative ease into any subject of thought, and of taking up with
aptitude any science or profession.[24]

Pointing out that the *Discourses* "are directed simply to the
consideration of the *aims* and *principles* of Education," Newman excuses himself from entering into practicalities ("the
true *mode* of educating") but contents himself with the following fairly lengthy statement of method, which he would elaborate later in great detail in one of the *Lectures and Essays:*

> Suffice it, then, to say here, that I hold very strongly that the
> first step in intellectual training is to impress upon a boy's mind
> the idea of science, method, order, principle, and system; of rule
> and exception, of richness and harmony. This is commonly and
> excellently done by making him begin with Grammar; nor can
> too great accuracy, or minuteness and subtlety of teaching be
> used towards him, as his faculties expand, with this simple pur-
> pose. Hence it is that critical scholarship is so important a disci-
> pline for him when he is leaving school for the University. A
> second science is the Mathematics: this should follow Grammar,
> still with the same subject, viz., to give him a conception of
> development and arrangement from and around a common cen-
> tre. Hence it is that Chronology and Geography are so necessary
> for him, when he reads History, which is otherwise little better
> than a storybook. Hence, too, Metrical Composition, when he
> reads Poetry; in order to stimulate his powers into action in every
> practicable way, and to prevent a merely passive reception of
> images and ideas which in that case are likely to pass out of the
> mind as soon as they have entered it. Let him once gain this
> habit of method, of starting from fixed points, of making his
> ground good as he goes, of distinguishing what he knows from
> what he does not know, and I conceive he will be gradually
> initiated into the largest and truest philosophical views, and will
> feel nothing but impatience and disgust at the random theories
> and imposing sophistries and dashing paradoxes, which carry
> away half-formed and superficial intellects.[25]

It is noticeable how Newman says nothing here about the actual acquisition of knowledge, scientific or otherwise, or of the appreciation of the arts—important, of course, as he thought both to be. Rather, the entire emphasis falls on training the mind to be accurate, consistent, logical, orderly. And at the end of the passage just quoted, he surely makes it quite clear that what he calls "a science of sciences" or "Philosophy"[26] is not a further subject in the curriculum, nor is it some kind of supergeneral science which embraces all the other sciences: on the contrary, far from being a subject you can study, it is only as a result of learning to think properly that one is "gradually initiated into the largest and truest philosophical views." In other words, the more the mind is formed and trained, the more "philosophical" it becomes.

It is not only in the Preface that Newman resists hyperbole: in the fifth Discourse, for example, he states simply and unequivocally: "Surely it is very intelligible to say . . . that Liberal Education, viewed in itself, is simply the cultivation of the intellect, as such, and its object is nothing more or less than intellectual excellence."[27] At the beginning of the next Discourse he laments that there is no recognized English word to express the idea of intellectual cultivation or the cultivated intellect:

It were well if the English, like the Greek language, possessed some definite word to express, simply and generally, intellectual proficiency or perfection, such as "health," as used with reference to the animal frame, and "virtue," with reference to our moral nature. I am not able to find such a term;—talent, ability, genius, belong distinctly to the raw material, which is the subject-matter, not to that excellence which is the result of exercise and training. When we turn, indeed, to the particular kinds of intellectual perfection, words are forthcoming for our purpose, as, for instance, judgment, taste, and skill; yet even these belong, for the most part, to powers or habits bearing upon practice or upon art, and not to any perfect condition of the intellect, considered in itself. Wisdom, again, is certainly a more comprehensive word than any other, but it has a direct relation to conduct, and to human life. Knowledge, indeed, and Science express purely intellectual ideas, but still not a state or quality of the intellect; for knowledge, in its ordinary sense, is but one of its circumstances, denoting a possession or a habit; and science has been appropriated to the subject-matter of the intellect, instead of belonging in English, as it ought to do, to the intellect itself.[28]

One modern commentator has expressed surprise that "Newman does not meet the want of 'some definite word' with the word 'culture.' . . . Elsewhere, he in fact made the essential connexion with 'culture.'"[29] In the passage referred to, Newman does indeed speak of "intellectual culture," but it is synonymous with what he calls "the culture of the intellect," whereby the intellect is "exercised in order to its perfect state."[30] Certainly Matthew Arnold, from whom the word *culture* in its usual modern sense derives, did not define culture as a state of "intellectual perfection," but rather as "a pursuit of our total perfection." The word *culture* for Arnold not only meant a "pursuit" rather than a "state," but its connotations are not even primarily, let alone exclusively, intellectual: "culture being a pursuit of our total perfection by means of getting to know . . . the best which has been thought and said in the world."[31] This indeed is what is generally meant by a liberal education, but it is not what Newman meant: for him "intellectual culture" did not mean reading "great books," but learning how to think. Newman's failure, then, to use the word *culture* in the sixth Discourse was no oversight on his part, but it did result in his adopting a terminology which may be confusing to us today: "In default of a recognized term, I have called the perfection or virtue of the intellect by the name of philosophy, philosophical knowledge, enlargement of mind, or illumination. . . ."[32]

This training of the mind does not consist either in studying logic or in the study of "how to think": one learns to think not by learning a science of thinking but by thinking about the ordinary subjects of knowledge. This is why, Newman says, "philosophy presupposes knowledge" and "requires a great deal of reading," for knowledge "is the indispensable condition of expansion of mind, and the instrument of attaining to it."[33] But the knowledge is strictly distinguished from the philosophy: merely to know is not to be educated:

> The enlargement consists, not merely in the passive reception into the mind of a number of ideas hitherto unknown to it, but in the mind's energetic and simultaneous action upon and towards and among those new ideas, which are rushing in upon it. . . . There is no enlargement, unless there be a comparison of ideas one with another, as they come before the mind, and a systematizing of them. . . . It is not the mere addition to our knowledge that is the illumination; but the locomotion, the movement onwards, of that mental centre, to which both what we know, and what we are learning, the accumulating mass of our acquirements, gravitates.[34]

This philosophy or enlargement of mind is not something absolute but admits of degrees. Thus, Newman adds here, "a truly great intellect . . . possesses the knowledge, not only of things, but also of their mutual and true relations," for

> That only is true enlargement of mind which is the power of viewing many things at once as one whole, of referring them severally to their true place in the universal system, of understanding their respective values, and determining their mutual dependence. Thus is that form of Universal Knowledge, of which I have on a former occasion spoken, set up in the individual intellect, and constitutes its perfection. Possessed of this real illumination, the mind never views any part of the extended subject-matter of Knowledge without recollecting that it is but a part, or without the associations which spring from this recollection. It makes every thing in some sort lead to every thing else; it would communicate the image of the whole to every separate portion, till that whole becomes in imagination like a spirit, every where pervading and penetrating its component parts, and

giving them one definite meaning. Just as our bodily organs, when mentioned, recall their function in the body, as the word "creation" suggests the Creator, and "subjects" a sovereign, so, in the mind of the Philosopher, as we are abstractedly conceiving of him, the elements of the physical and moral world, sciences, arts, pursuits, ranks, offices, events, opinions, individualities, are all viewed as one, with correlative functions, and as gradually by successive combinations converging, one and all, to the true centre.[35]

The word *abstractedly* again reminds us that Newman is speaking in idealistic, not to say hyperbolic, terms. The ideal "Philosopher" he evokes here is simply the most highly educated and intelligent person it is possible to conceive of. He is certainly not necessarily a genius in philosophy in the academic sense of the word. Indeed, Newman's "Philosopher" is not a genius at all in the normal sense of the word:

There are men who, when in difficulties, originate at the moment vast ideas or dazzling projects; who, under the influence of excitement, are able to cast a light, almost as if from inspiration, on a subject or course of action which comes before them; who have a sudden presence of mind equal to any emergency, rising with the occasion, and an undaunted magnanimous bearing, and an energy and keenness which is but made intense by opposition. This is genius, this is heroism; it is the exhibition of a natural gift, which no culture can teach, at which no Institution can aim; here, on the contrary, we are concerned, not with mere nature, but with training and teaching. That perfection of the Intellect, which is the result of Education, and its *beau ideal*, to be imparted to individuals in their respective measures, is the clear, calm, accurate vision and comprehension of all things, as far as the finite mind can embrace them, each in its place, and with its own characteristics upon it. It is almost prophetic from its knowledge of history; it is almost heart-searching from its knowledge of human nature; it has almost supernatural charity from its freedom from littleness and prejudice; it has almost the repose of faith, because nothing can startle it; it has almost the beauty and harmony of heavenly contemplation, so intimate is it with the eternal order of things and the music of the spheres.

Whereas the mind of a genius tends to be "possessed with some one object," to "take exaggerated views of its importance," to be "feverish in the pursuit of it," and to "make it the measure of things which are utterly foreign to it"—the educated mind, "which has been disciplined to the perfection of its powers, which knows, and thinks while it knows, which has learned to leaven the dense mass of facts and events with the elastic force of reason, such an intellect cannot be partial, cannot be exclusive, cannot be impetuous, cannot be at a loss, cannot but be patient, collected, and majestically calm, because it discerns the end in every beginning, the origin in every end, the law in every interruption, the limit in each delay; because it ever knows where it stands and how its path lies from one point to another."[36] This kind of "litany" surely makes only too obvious the element of hyperbole, which, sincere as it is, is not to be taken too literally, as the explicit religious analogies (at the end of the long passage just quoted) also make clear, for Newman is the very last person to place religious faith on the same level as secular education.

Newman is eloquent on the danger of emphasizing the sheer acquisition of knowledge at the expense of genuine education. Arguing that "if we would improve the intellect, first of all, we must ascend; we cannot gain real knowledge on a level; we must generalize, we must reduce to method, we must have a grasp of principles, and group and shape our acquisitions by means of them," he uses some vividly concrete imagery which reflects his own personal concern always to have a "view" when confronted by a mass of information: "Who has not felt the irritation of mind and impatience created by a deep, rich country, visited for the first time, with winding lanes, and high hedges, and green steeps, and tangled woods, and every thing smiling indeed, but in a maze? The same feeling comes upon us in a strange city, when we have no map of its streets." And he warns that memory (which "can tyrannize") may be "over-stimulated," so that "Reason acts almost as feebly and as impotently as in the madman" when the intellect is "the prey . . . of barren facts, of random intrusions from without." But, he complains, the "practical error" of modern education is, "not to load the memory of the student with a mass of undigested knowledge, but to force upon him so much that he has rejected all. It has been the error of distracting and enfeebling the mind by an unmeaning profusion of subjects; of implying that a smattering in a dozen branches of study is not shallowness, which it really is, but enlargement, which it is not. . . ." And he prefers specialization to a more general course of studies if there has to be a choice between a "thorough knowledge of one science" and "a superficial acquaintance with many," for "a smattering of a hundred things" does not lead to "a philosophical or comprehensive view" (any more than does mere "memory for detail").

A reference to the rise of modern technology provides something more than an analogy: "What the steam engine does with matter, the printing press is to do with mind; it is to act mechanically, and the population is to be passively, almost unconsciously enlightened, by the mere multiplication and dissemination of volumes." The opposite of the mechanical is the "individual" element—"the power of initiation"—which Newman regards as essential to education: for one can only become educated by actively using one's own mind oneself as opposed to passively absorbing information. As our jargon today would put it, what is received "externally" has to be "internalized" for it to become an integral part of the person learning. Newman makes the point in his own ironic way: "Learning is to be without exertion, without attention, without toil; without grounding, without advance, without finishing." However, he is not against the spread of popular education through "the cheap publication of scientific and literary works, which is now in vogue," and as for that "superficial" general knowledge "which periodical literature and occasional lectures and scientific institutions diffuse through the community," he accepts that it is even "a necessary accomplishment, in the case of educated men." What he does not accept is that such proliferation of information—and we would have to include educational programs on television—actually educates people: "accomplishments are not education" for they do not "form or cultivate the intellect."[37]

Once again we note that Newman's idea of a liberal education is very different from what is often understood to be equivalent to a liberal education: indeed, the very notion of a degree in "general studies," insofar as it implies an inevitably superficial knowledge of a number of more or less disconnected subjects, is the antithesis of Newman's idea. To impart knowledge in as many different areas as possible is no more to educate, in Newman's sense, than to instill an appreciation of the arts. The point is not that Newman is against knowing as much as possible about as many branches of knowledge as possible or that he is in any way adverse to a knowledge of the arts (which, of course, he is not), but that neither by or in itself constitutes what he means by real education, namely, the training of the mind and the development of the intellectual powers.

The stark contrast that Newman draws between a university which provides instruction but not education and a university which offers virtually no formal instruction but which, in spite of itself, does make possible some kind of an education, not only serves as an extreme statement of his case, but introduces an important and essential facet of Newman's conception of an education which constitutes a real training of the mind.

I protest . . . that if I had to choose between a so-called University, which dispensed with residence and tutorial superintendence, and gave its degrees to any person who passed an examination in a wide range of subjects, and a University which had no professors or examinations at all, but merely brought a number of young men together for three or four years, and then sent them away as the University of Oxford is said to have done some sixty years since, if I were asked which of these two methods were the better discipline of the intellect . . . if I must determine which of the two courses was the more successful in training, moulding, enlarging the mind . . . I have no hesitation in giving the preference to that University which did nothing, over that which exacted of its members an acquaintance with every science under the sun.

The reason is that the one university (Oxford) offered a residential setting where an intellectual or learning environment was at least possible and the other (London) does not because it is nonresidential.

When a multitude of young men . . . come together and freely mix with each other, they are sure to learn one from another, even if there be no one to teach them; the conversation of all is a series of lectures to each, and they gain for themselves new ideas and views, fresh matter of thought, and distinct principles for judging and acting, day by day.

In other words, where there is no academic community—what Newman elsewhere calls an "atmosphere of intellect"[38]—students will inevitably argue and discuss among themselves, so that they in effect help to train each other's minds.

Here then is a real teaching . . . it at least tends towards cultivation of the intellect; it at least recognizes that knowledge is something more than a sort of passive reception of scraps and details; it is a something, and it does a something, which never will issue from the most strenuous efforts of a set of teachers, with no mutual sympathies and no intercommunion, of a set of examiners with no opinions which they dare profess, and with no common principles, who are teaching or questioning a set of youths who do not know them, and do not know each other, on a large number of subjects, different in kind, and connected by no wide philosophy, three times a week, or three times a year, or once in three years, in chill lecture-rooms or on a pompous anniversary.[39]

Not only that, but this "youthful community" gradually acquires a corporate character of its own which itself exerts a formative educational influence:

> [it] will constitute a whole, it will embody a specific idea, it will represent a doctrine, it will administer a code of conduct, and it will furnish principles of thought and action. It will give birth to a living teaching, which in course of time will take the shape of a self-perpetuating tradition, or a *genius loci*, as it is sometimes called; which haunts the home where it has been born, and which imbues and forms, more or less, and one by one, every individual who is successively brought under its shadow.

Such "self-education in any shape," Newman insists, "in the most restricted sense, is preferable to a system of teaching which, professing so much, really does so little for the mind." For in spite of all the imperfections and limitations of self-educated minds, which he catalogues relentlessly, "they are likely to have more thought, more mind, more philosophy, more true enlargement, than those earnest but ill-used persons, who are forced to load their minds with a score of subjects against an examination, who have too much on their hands to indulge themselves in thinking or investigation, who devour premiss and conclusion together with indiscriminate greediness, who hold whole sciences on faith, and commit demonstrations to memory, and who too often, as might be expected, when their period of education is passed, throw up all they have learned in disgust, having gained nothing really by their anxious labours, except perhaps the habit of application." Indeed, concludes Newman, and without any hyperbole, it would be far better not to go to university, "than to submit to a drudgery so ignoble, a mockery so contumelious! How much more profitable for the independent mind, after the mere rudiments of education, to range through a library at random, taking down books as they meet him, and pursuing the trains of thought which his mother wit suggests!" It is not that he is against students having to work and pass examinations, but he is profoundly hostile to any system which leaves the students "simply dissipated and relaxed by the multiplicity of subjects, which they have never really mastered, and so shallow as not even to know their shallowness." It is something surely of a paradox that *The Idea of a University* should state so unequivocally that somebody who has never studied at a university may well gain a "more genuine" education than many a university graduate.[40]

To suppose that for Newman the well-trained mind is simply the mind that is clear in argument and investigation would be to limit his conception of a liberal education. What he calls "the cultivation of the intellect" or the "scientific formation of mind" does indeed result in the ability to "grasp things as they are" and the "power of discriminating between truth and falsehood"; but it also includes the capacity "of arranging things according to their real value." It is not only a matter of "clearsightedness," since the "sagacity" or "wisdom" which the educated person is supposed to possess involves too "an acquired faculty of judgment." In other words, Newman is desiderating not only clear thinking but also the power of evaluating and of making normative judgments. Thus, while logical lucidity is an essential attribute of the educated mind, so too is the power of distinguishing priorities, of seeing what is important and significant and what is not, of making the kind of evaluations that will certainly greatly vary from subject to subject in their "ethical" content (or lack of) but which are inseparable from the decision-making which is inherent in all acquisitions of and advances in knowledge.

The mind for Newman does not consist only in the logical faculty: he warns that just "as some member or organ of the body may be inordinately used and developed, so may memory, or imagination, or the reasoning faculty." And "*this*," he insists, "is not intellectual culture." But rather, "as the body may be tended, cherished, and exercised with a simple view to its general health, so may the intellect also be generally exercised in order to its perfect state; and this *is* its cultivation." It is clear that the mind can only be logical so far as imagination and memory provide the materials for it to be logical about. Again, without the evaluative and judgmental element, it is hard to see how the mind can come to decisions, however clear and lucid it may be in its thought-processes. The academic, to take a rather specialized example of the educated man, knows "where he and his science stand" because "he has come to it, as it were, from a height, he has taken a survey of all knowledge . . . and he treats his own in consequence with a philosophy and a resource, which belongs not to the study itself, but to his liberal education." It is evident that it is not clear thinking alone which enables him to do so, but the ability amongst others, to make normative discriminations and judgments. The fact that clear-headedness, although for Newman undoubtedly the most important and the absolutely indispensable end of education, is not enough, is shown by, for example, his remark that it is a liberal education which "gives a man a clear conscious view of his own opinions and judgments, a truth in developing them, an eloquence in expressing them, and a force in urging them."[41] It is obvious that an eloquent presentation of an argument or case demands some use of the imagination, for instance.

The theory of a liberal education which we have been tracing through the *Discourses* is exemplified in an extremely concrete way in "Elementary Studies," one of the *Lectures and Essays* which constitute the second half of *The Idea of a University*. As the title suggests, however, it is not concerned with university studies but with the kind of education suitable for those intending to go to university. Newman begins by stressing that very clearmindedness which we have seen lies at the heart of his view of a liberal education:

> I say, that one main portion of intellectual education, of the labours of both school and university, is to remove the original dimness of the mind's eye; to strengthen and perfect its vision; to enable it to look out into the world right forward, steadily and truly; to give the mind clearness, accuracy, precision; to enable it to use words aright, to understand what it says, to conceive

justly what it thinks about, to abstract, compare, analyze, divide, define, and reason, correctly.

We notice that Newman carefully says that this training of the mind to think accurately and logically is only "one main portion of intellectual education." As we have seen, there are other parts of the mind which also need developing. The point that learning to think logically is not the same as learning the subject called "logic" is now made explicit:

> There is a particular science which takes these matters in hand, and it is called logic; but it is not by logic, certainly not by logic alone, that the faculty I speak of is acquired. The infant does not learn to spell and read the hues upon his retina by any scientific rule; nor does the student learn accuracy of thought by any manual or treatise. The instruction given him, of whatever kind, if it be really instruction, is mainly, or at least pre-eminently, this,—a discipline in accuracy of mind.

Again Newman makes it clear that this "accuracy of mind," although not the whole purpose of education, has priority over all other considerations; and again he stresses that the formally uneducated may be better educated in this sense than the formally educated:

> It is this haziness of intellectual vision which is the malady of all classes of men by nature, of those who read and write and compose, quite as well as of those who cannot,—of all who have not had a really good education. Those who cannot either read or write may, nevertheless, be in the number of those who have remedied and got rid of it; those who can, are too often still under its power. It is an acquisition quite separate from miscellaneous information, or knowledge of books.

The great practical "maxim" of the teacher should be

> "a little, but well"; that is, really know what you say you know: know what you know and what you do not know; get one thing well before you go on to a second; try to ascertain what your words mean; when you read a sentence, picture it before your

mind as a whole, take in the truth or information contained in it, express it in your own words, and, if it be important, commit it to the faithful memory. Again, compare one idea with another; adjust truths and facts; form them into one whole, or notice the obstacles which occur in doing so. This is the way to make progress; this is the way to arrive at results; not to swallow knowledge, but . . . to masticate and digest it.[42]

In a passage like this we may seem very far away from the elevated generalities of the Discourses, and yet it is quite clear that "Elementary Studies" is a practical application of the theory of the Discourses. Indeed, the relentlessly detailed practicalities help to place any potentially misleading hyperbole in the Discourses in its true perspective and to link it firmly with the initial position set out in the Preface, namely, that the purpose of a university education is "real cultivation of mind," that is, "the intellect . . . properly trained and formed to have a connected view or grasp of things."[43]

Elsewhere in the Lectures and Essays Newman's central educational theme—as opposed to the religious and theological considerations involved in the founding and organization of a Catholic university—is further elucidated and substantiated. Thus in "University Preaching," he points out that

writing is a stimulus to the mental faculties, to the logical talent, to originality, to the power of illustration, to the arrangement of topics, second to none. Till a man begins to put down his thoughts about a subject on paper he will not ascertain what he knows and what he does not know; and still less will he be able to express what he does know.[44]

If one fundamental principle for Newman is that the student must write essays or papers, and not merely take notes, another is that the university teacher is not there simply to lecture. In "Discipline of Mind," he first reiterates that learning is not a solely passive process:

A man may hear a thousand lectures, and read a thousand volumes, and be at the end of the process very much where he was, as regards knowledge. Something more than merely *admitting* it in a negative way into the mind is necessary, if it is to remain there. It must not be passively received, but actually and actively entered into, embraced, mastered. The mind must go half-way to meet what comes to it from without.[45]

Or, as he puts it in "Elementary Studies," "you must not trust to books, but only make use of them; not hang like a dead weight upon your teacher, but catch some of his life; handle what is given you, not as a formula, but as a pattern to copy and as a capital to improve; throw your heart and mind into what you are about, and thus unite the separate advantages of being tutored and of being self-taught. . . ."[46] But, as he goes on to insist in "Discipline of Mind," the teacher has a responsibility to make sure that teaching is not merely lecturing by rote; some kind of conversation or dialogue between teacher and taught is integral to true education:

> You do not come merely to hear a lecture, or to read a book, but you come for that catechetical instruction, which consists in a sort of conversation between your lecturer and you. He tells you a thing, and he asks you to repeat it after him. He questions you, he examines you, he will not let you go till he has a proof, not only that you have heard, but that you know.

That Newman has in mind something rather more rigorous than some kind of vague, open-ended discussion or exchange of views is made even more obvious by yet another reiteration of the central thesis of the *Idea*. "I consider, then, that the position of our minds, as far as they are uncultivated, towards intellectual objects,—I mean of our minds, before they have been disciplined and formed by the action of our reason upon them,—is analogous to that of a blind man towards the objects of vision, at the moment when eyes are for the first time given to him by the skill of the operator." Clear thinking and understanding are what education is about: "how many disputes," Newman says, are "interminable, because neither party understood either his opponent or himself." For, he explains with another analogy from sight, "many a man considers a mere hazy view of many things to be real knowledge, whereas it does but mislead, just as a short-sighted man sees only so far as to be led by his uncertain sight over the precipice." On the other hand, "true cultivation of mind" comes from thorough study of a subject, "it does not matter what it is, if it be really studied and mastered, as far as it is taken up":

> The result is a formation of mind,—that is, a habit of order and system, a habit of referring every accession of knowledge to what we already know, and of adjusting the one with the other; and, moreover, as such a habit implies, the actual acceptance and use of certain principles as centres of thought, around which our knowledge grows and is located. . . . This is that faculty of perception in intellectual matters, which, as I have said so often, is analogous to the capacity we all have of mastering the multitude of lines and colours which pour in upon our eyes, and of deciding what every one of them is worth.[47]

If we turn from Newman's concept of a liberal education to his idea of the university that is to provide it, we find again an element of hyperbole which should not be allowed to confuse the principle at issue. The Preface to the *Discourses* begins with the uncompromising statement that a university "is a place of *teaching* universal *knowledge*."[48] Now this may seem an obviously impractical aspiration, or indeed a less than desirable ideal. For not only would it appear in practice to be impossible for any one university "to profess all branches of knowledge,"[49] but the very attempt may be thought to be a highly distracting and futile exercise calculated to dissipate energies that could be better concentrated and directed to more restricted and realizable goals. Once again Newman must not be taken too literally. His own university in Dublin did not in fact teach all conceivable branches of knowledge, nor is there any sign that its Rector did not regard it as a proper university because, for example, there was no chair of Chinese studies. Stripped of its rhetorical hyperbole, Newman's point is really the negative insistence that a university should not refuse to countenance any particular area of knowledge by in effect discriminating against it—"through the systematic omission of any one science."[50] Clearly he would have regarded certain fundamental subjects—including theology—as absolutely indispensable, but it is ludicrous to suppose that he wanted a university to include every conceivable branch of knowledge known to man. In fact, in the last of the *Discourses* he makes the necessary modification when he states that "all branches of knowledge are, at least implicitly, the subject-matter of its teaching."[51] In other words, a university must be in principle hospitable and in practice not hostile to any kind of knowledge. What subjects a university explicitly teaches will depend on a number of educational and practical factors; but implicitly it is ready to teach any genuine branch of knowledge because by its very definition a university cannot exclude or refuse to recognize any part of human knowledge.

Of course, Newman's insistence on the intellectual catholicity of a university arises out of his argument for the study of theology, but its importance extends far beyond the particular case in question. It is not an unrealistic and pointless ideal that is being advocated, but rather a principle which is vital for the freedom and integrity of the university. There must be no curtailments or restrictions, reflecting any dogmatic or narrow or specialized conceptions of the range of human knowledge. "For instance, are we to limit our idea of University Knowledge by the evidence of our senses? then we exclude ethics; by intuition? we exclude history; by testimony? we exclude metaphysics; by abstract reasoning? we exclude physics."[52] Rather, Newman insists not only on the fullness but on the wholeness and unity of knowledge:

All that exists, as contemplated by the human mind, forms one large system or complex fact, and this of course resolves itself into an indefinite number of particular facts, which, as being portions of a whole, have countless relations of every kind, one towards another. Knowledge is the apprehension of these facts, whether in themselves, or in their mutual positions and bearings. And, as all taken together form one integral subject for contemplation, so there are no natural or real limits between part and part; one is ever running into another; all, as viewed by the mind, are combined together, and possess a correlative character one with another. . . .[53]

The reason why "all knowledge forms one whole" is that

its subject-matter is one; for the universe in its length and breadth is so intimately knit together, that we cannot separate off portion from portion, and operation from operation, except by a mental abstraction. . . . Next, sciences are the results of that mental abstraction. . . . being the logical record of this or that aspect of the whole subject-matter of knowledge. As they all belong to one and the same circle of objects, they are one and all connected together; as they are but aspects of things, they are severally incomplete in their relation to the things themselves, though complete in their own idea and for their own respective purposes; on both accounts they at once need and subserve each other.[54]

A university may not in practice (explicitly) teach all the branches of knowledge, but in theory (implicitly) it must be open to doing so, for if they "all relate to one and the same integral subject-matter . . . none can safely be omitted, if we would obtain the exactest knowledge possible of things as they are, and . . . the omission is more or less important, in proportion to the field which each covers, and the depth to which it penetrates, and the order to which it belongs; for its loss is a positive privation of an influence which exerts itself in the correction and completion of the rest."[55]

Newman's view of the interaction and interdependence of the various branches of knowledge is important both for his idea of a university as an institution and for his conception of a liberal education. First, his commitment to the integrity of knowledge leads him to point out the danger of one branch of knowledge intruding into the sphere of another. Different branches of knowledge "differ in importance; and according to their importance will be their influence, not only on the mass of knowledge to which they all converge and contribute, but on each other." We have seen that Newman is in favor of "specialization" to the extent that he is against any kind of superficial smattering of knowledge. What, however, he is very hostile to is the specialization of those specialists who regard their own speciality as the key to other knowledge and thus "necessarily become bigots and quacks, scorning all principles and reported facts which do not belong to their own pursuit." For in the "whole circle of sciences, one corrects another for purposes of fact, and one without the other cannot dogmatize, except hypothetically and upon its own abstract principles." Thus, for example, a sociologist or a moral philosopher may find a work of fiction to be of great sociological or philosophical interest, but its artistic significance is a matter for the literary critic, and, however rich in information about society or pregnant with ethical problems, it may still be a very poor work of fiction. Conversely, a novel may be misleading as a document of social history or philosophically uninteresting and yet be a great work of literature. Newman's insistence that the various "sciences" only study their own particular aspects of reality is perennially valid, as each age tends to exalt and exaggerate whatever branch of knowledge happens to be predominant or in fashion and as each specialized branch of knowledge tends to view the world from its own limited vantage point.

> [S]ciences are the . . . record of this or that aspect of the whole subject-matter of knowledge. As they all belong to one and the same circle of objects, they are one and all connected together; as they are but aspects of things, they are severally incomplete in their relation to the things themselves, though complete in their own idea and for their own respective purposes; on both accounts they at once need and subserve each other.[56]

Newman is emphatic that the neglect or omission of any branch of knowledge, particularly if it is important and likely to impinge on other branches, does not mean that that subject simply slips out of the totality of knowledge—for

> if you drop any science out of the circle of knowledge, you cannot keep its place vacant for it; that science is forgotten; the other sciences close up, or, in other words, they exceed their proper bounds, and intrude where they have no right. For instance, I suppose, if ethics were sent into banishment, its territory would soon disappear, under a treaty of partition, as it may be called, between law, political economy, and physiology. . . .[57]

The more specialized somebody's field of knowledge is, the more likely, Newman argues, is this kind of academic imperialism to manifest itself:

> in proportion to the narrowness of his knowledge, is, not his distrust of it, but the deep hold it has upon him, his absolute conviction of his own conclusions, and his positiveness in maintaining them. . . . Thus he becomes, what is commonly called, a man of one idea; which properly means a man of one science, and of the view, partly true, but subordinate, partly false, which is all that can proceed out of any thing so partial. Hence it is that we have the principles of utility, of combination, of progress, of philanthropy, or, in material sciences, comparative anatomy, phrenology, electricity, exalted into leading ideas, and keys, if not of all knowledge, at least of many things more than belong to them. . . .[58]

In our own time we might cite the rise of sociology as a social science and its consequent intrusion into the areas of, for example, ethics, theology, and literature, when sociological criteria and norms are used to criticize and evaluate data (which may indeed bear a sociological analysis) in such a way as to suggest that other (ethical, theological, and literary) interpretations are irrelevant or redundant or unnecessary. Such sociologists, to use Newman's words, "have made their own science . . . the centre of all truth, and view every part or the chief parts of knowledge as if developed from it, and to be tested and determined by its principles."[59]

When it comes actually to evaluating the different branches of knowledge themselves, Newman makes the pertinent point that the particular science is hardly in a position to evaluate itself *qua* branch of knowledge. Thus "if there is a science of wealth, it must give rules for gaining wealth and disposing of wealth," but it "can do nothing more; it cannot itself declare that it is a subordinate science." The economist, Newman declares roundly, has no business "to recommend the science of wealth, by claiming for it an *ethical* quality, viz., by extolling it as the road to virtue and happiness." Such an evaluation must either come from those branches of knowledge which are specifically concerned with ethical and teleological questions or must ultimately be made not by any particular branch of knowledge but by the trained "philosophical" mind itself:

> The objection that Political Economy is inferior to the science of virtue, or does not conduce to happiness, is an ethical or theological objection; the question of its "rank" belongs to that Architectonic Science or Philosophy, whatever it be, which is itself the arbiter of all truth, and which disposes of the claims and arranges the places of all the departments of knowledge which man is able to master.[60]

But even apart from the status of economics as a science, questions of value inevitably enter into the study of economics whether as ethical or political issues, which the economist may be tempted to settle *qua* economist by treating them as if they were economic rather than ethical or political problems. Thus, for example, an economist may argue for a socialist as opposed to monetarist economic policy on the concealed ethical or political premiss—which is outside the scope of economics—that it is preferable, from the egalitarian point of view, that all the slices of the national economic cake should be as near as possible in size even if this means that the smallest slices will in fact be smaller than in a less evenly divided cake. It is because "the various branches of science are intimately connected with each other"[61] that it is impossible to proceed very far in economics without being confronted by ethical or political factors. These cannot be determined by economic criteria, nor should they be covertly settled by the economist's own private ethical or political views. Dramatic developments in the experimental or technological sciences have led to such dangerous threats to the very existence and foundations of human life that scientists nowadays are increasingly sensitive to moral and even religious questions which they are well aware fall outside their competence as scientists. Perhaps the temptation to encroach on other fields is less obvious in the arts and social sciences. At any rate the fundamental principle is clearly stated by Newman: "What is true in one science is dictated to us indeed according to that science, but not according to another science, or in another department." The conflict may arise out of the simple fact that one science takes precedence over another: thus, for example, military science "must ever be subordinate to political considerations or maxims of government, which is a higher science with higher objects."[62]

The danger in Newman's eyes is accentuated if the academic is outside the community of a university, because then

> he is in danger of being absorbed and narrowed by his pursuit, and of giving Lectures which are the Lectures of nothing more than a lawyer, physician, geologist, or political economist; whereas in a University he will just know where he and his science stand, he has come to it, as it were, from a height, he has taken a survey of all knowledge, he is kept from extravagance by the very rivalry of other studies, he has gained from them a special illumination and largeness of mind and freedom and self-possession, and he treats his own in consequence with a philosophy and a resource, which belongs not to the study itself, but to his liberal education.[63]

The problem is also a problem for the student who needs to be reminded at the university of the whole circle of knowledge. "There is no science but tells a different tale, when viewed as a portion of a whole, from what it is likely to suggest when taken by itself, without the safeguard, as I may call it, of others." This, of course, is the danger of specialization: "If his reading is confined simply to one subject . . . certainly it has a tendency to contract his mind." On the other hand, "the drift and meaning of a branch of knowledge varies with the company in which it is introduced to the student," so it is important what subjects are studied with what. Newman has no intention of advocating that a student should attempt to study every subject, but he is insistent that a student should be aware of as many academic horizons as possible:

> It is a great point then to enlarge the range of studies which a University professes, even for the sake of the students; and, though they cannot pursue every subject which is open to them, they will be the gainers by living among those and under those who represent the whole circle. This I conceive to be the advantage of a seat of learning, considered as a place of education. An assemblage of learned men, zealous for their own sciences, and rivals of each other, are brought, by familiar intercourse and for the sake of intellectual peace, to adjust together the claims and relations of their respective subjects of investigation. They learn to respect, to consult, to aid each other. Thus is created a pure and clear atmosphere of thought, which the student also breathes, though in his own case he only pursues a few sciences out of the multitude. He profits by an intellectual tradition, which is independent of particular teachers, which guides him in his choice of subjects, and duly interprets for him those which he chooses. He apprehends the great outlines of knowledge, the principles on which it rests, the scale of its parts, its lights and its shades, its great points and its little, as he otherwise cannot apprehend them. Hence it is that his education is called "Liberal." A habit of mind is formed which lasts through life, of which the attributes are, freedom, equitableness, calmness, moderation, and wisdom; or what . . . I have ventured to call a philosophical habit.[64]

We may think there is an element of hyperbole in this evocation of a university education, but Newman's essential point
is surely clear enough and well-founded: because, in the right
kind of academic environment, students meet and mix with
each other, it makes quite a lot of difference whether, as in
some institutions of higher education, all the students are
studying the same subject, be it art or music or engineering
or medicine, or whether students are in contact with other
students studying a variety of subjects. Ideally, there would
be some influence (something would "rub off"), but at the
very least there would be a real awareness of other intellectual
ways of life.

Newman was keenly aware of the actual real-life context
of the university in which both teaching and learning take
place. Like other communities and institutions, universities
inevitably have a "spirit" of their own and "since they are
living and energizing bodies . . . of necessity have some one
formal and definite ethical character, good or bad, and do of
a certainty imprint that character on the individuals who
direct and who frequent them."[65] In many ways Newman's
idea of the university resembles his idea of the Church. Both
are essentially communities made up of living people and with
a living tradition, but both also have an institutional aspect,
if only because some members of the community exercise the
role of authority. As a result, just as the Church is an "authoritative" institution, so too is the university which not only
"occupies the whole territory of knowledge," but "is the very
realm," for "it professes much more than to take in and to
lodge as in a caravanserai all art and science, all history and
philosophy":

> In truth, it professes to assign to each study, which it receives,
> its own proper place and its just boundaries; to define the rights,
> to establish the mutual relations, and to effect the intercom-
> munion of one and all; to keep in check the ambitious and
> encroaching, and to succour and maintain those which from
> time to time are succumbing under the more popular or the more

fortunately circumstanced; to keep the peace between them all, and to convert their mutual differences and contrarieties into the common good. . . . Thus to draw many things into one, is its special function; and it learns to do it, not by rules reducible to writing, but by sagacity, wisdom, and forbearance, acting upon a profound insight into the subject-matter of knowledge, and by a vigilant repression of aggression or bigotry in any quarter. . . .

What an empire is in political history, such is a University in the sphere of philosophy and research. It is, as I have said, the high protecting power of all knowledge and science, of fact and principle, of inquiry and discovery, of experiment and specula-tion; it maps out the territory of the intellect, and sees that the boundaries of each province are religiously respected, and that there is neither encroachment nor surrender on any side. It acts as umpire between truth and truth, and, taking into account the nature and importance of each, assigns to all their due order of precedence. It maintains no one department of thought exclu-sively, however ample and noble; and it sacrifices none. It is deferential and loyal, according to their respective weight, to the claims of literature, of physical research, of history, of metaphys-ics, of theological science. It is impartial towards them all, and promotes each in its own place and for its own object. . . .

In this point of view, its several professors are like the minis-ters of various political powers at one court or conference. They represent their respective sciences, and attend to the private interests of those sciences respectively. . . . A liberal philosophy becomes the habit of minds thus exercised; a breadth and spa-ciousness of thought, in which lines, seemingly parallel, may converge at leisure, and principles, recognized as incommensura-ble, may be safely antagonistic. . . .

. . . the philosophy of an imperial intellect, for such I am considering a University to be, is based, not so much on simplifi-cation as on discrimination. Its true representative defines, rather than analyzes. He aims at no complete catalogue, or inter-pretation of the subjects of knowledge, but a following out, as far as man can, what in its fulness is mysterious and unfathomable. Taking into his charge all sciences, methods, collections of facts, principles, doctrines, truths, which are the reflexions of the universe upon the human intellect, he admits them all, he disregards none, and, as disregarding none, he allows none to exceed or encroach. His watchword is Live and let live. He takes things as they are; he submits to them all, as far as they go; he recognizes the insuperable lines of demarcation which run between subject and subject; he observes how separate truths lie relatively to each other, where they concur, where they part company, and where, being carried too far, they cease to be truths at all. It is his office to determine how much can be known in each province of thought; when we must be contented not to know; in what direction inquiry is hopeless, or on the other hand full of promise; where it gathers into coils insoluble by reason, where it is absorbed in mysteries, or runs into the abyss. It will be his care to be familiar with the signs of real and apparent difficulties, with the methods proper to particular subject-matters, what in each particular case are the limits of a rational scepticism, and what the claims of a peremptory faith. If he has one cardinal maxim in his philosophy, it is, that truth cannot be contrary to truth; if he has a second, it is, that truth often *seems* contrary to truth; and, if a third, it is the practical conclusion, that we must be patient with such appearances, and not be hasty to pronounce them to be really of a more formidable character.[66]

The *Lectures and Essays* may be more practical and specific than the *Discourses,* but nowhere else in the *Idea of a University* does Newman write with such eloquence of the university than in this great purple passage from "Christianity and Scientific Investigation." It was not written to be taken quite literally; that would be to miss the spirit of its idealism. But neither again is it to be discounted or dismissed as mere hyperbole. The splendid rhetoric celebrates Newman's vision of both the unity of knowledge and the integrity of its individual branches, a vision which culminates in a faith in the ultimate victory of truth. Ideals and visions are important for providing inspiration and setting standards to be aimed at, and should be judged by how real they are rather than by how practical they may or may not be.

What, in conclusion, are we to say about Newman's achievement—as educator rather than writer—in the *Idea of a University*? Three major themes, which are at least as significant today as in his time, may be singled out. First, the fundamental requirement that the university graduate should be able to think clearly and exactly seems even more essential, if anything, in our day: the spread of education, the proliferation of knowledge, as well as its increased specialization, the rise of mass communications in addition to the growth of the popular press familiar to Newman, and a democratic society with universal suffrage—all these factors have only enhanced the importance of what Newman has to say about the real education of the mind. Otherwise, education threatens to become an ever more narrowly specialized training in those branches of knowledge that modern technological society values, while at the same time the lack of an educated class capable of clear thinking and articulated criticism only augments the dangers of intellectual manipulation through the media on a scale hardly dreamed of a century ago.

Second, the stress Newman lays on the personal interaction between student and teacher and on the university as an intellectual community is one that should strongly appeal to a culture which speaks so much about the need for both community and the personal element, precisely because of the lack of either in modern industrialized society, which is both atomized and depersonalized. The "holistic" view that modern medicine, for example, takes of human beings is the same kind of educational theory that the *Idea of a University* puts forward: just as the psychological state of the physically sick person may be highly relevant to his or her recovery, quite apart from surgery and drugs, so too, the *Idea* insists, the whole mind needs to be educated through active participation in a community of intellectual formation, not just the memory through passive attendance on impersonal lectures. Such a context for learning is so vital for Newman that he is prepared if necessary to abandon the basic formalities of academic instruction in favor of an association, however informal, of actual individual minds personally interacting.

Third, Newman's preoccupation with the relations between individual branches of knowledge reveals a penetrating realism about the ways in which individual specialisms are apt to arrogate to themselves evaluations and judgments on matters which lie outside their sphere of competence—a tendency for which contemporary analogues are not hard to find. However idealistic, the vision of a university where the various branches of knowledge hold their due and proper ground compels attention because of the absolute commitment to the pursuit of knowledge and the equally firm faith in the power of truth. Ultimately, the *Idea of a University* continues to inspire and stimulate generations of readers by virtue of the very passion with which it evokes the wonder of the human mind's capacity to know and to know as part of a great living tradition and community of minds in the pursuit of truth.

2

THE PHILOSOPHER

Newman was much more prolific as a theologian than as a philosopher of religion, and yet the justification of religious belief always remained the subject which was closest to his heart and which was never far from his thoughts throughout his life. In the face of increasing secularization and unbelief, he came to feel that the fundamental religious problem of the modern age was the crisis of faith.

Newman first began to think seriously about the basic philosophical issues in 1821 when he was twenty. During the next four years he wrote a number of long letters to his younger brother, Charles, who had become skeptical about the claims of Christianity. As an Evangelical (as he then was), Newman at first took the usual line that religious truth can only be attained with due moral seriousness and sincerity. But in 1825 he developed this conventional apologetic approach by arguing that "the rejection of Christianity" rose "from a fault of the *heart*, not of the *intellect*," since a "dislike of the *contents* of Scripture is at the bottom of unbelief." This was how he explained the fact that "the most powerful arguments for Christianity do not *convince*, only *silence*; for there is at the bottom that secret antipathy for the doctrines of Christianity, which is quite out of the reach of argument." This early, penetrating letter shows Newman already probing beneath the surface of explicit and ostensible arguments to find the real reasons why people believe and argue as they do: "We survey

moral and religious subjects through the glass of previous habits; and scarcely two persons use a glass of the same magnifying
power. I venture confidently to say, that if the contents of a
professed revelation on divine things are to be made the test
of its genuineness, *no revelation could* be made us; for scarcely
two persons can be got together, who will agree in their antecedent or self-originated ideas of God and his purposes towards man." It is therefore on its "credentials" or "claims,"
not its contents, that Christianity must be judged.[1]

This kind of realism was to characterize Newman's whole
approach to the philosophy of religion. He was to condemn,
for example, Locke's "view of the human mind" as "theoretical
and unreal . . . because he consults his own ideal of how the
mind ought to act, instead of interrogating human nature, as
an existing thing, as it is found in the world."[2] Newman's own
starting point was not a defense of belief in God or the Christian revelation, but rather an examination of the actual mental process by virtue of which somebody is a believer or an
unbeliever. What is it that really determines whether a person
believes or does not believe? Not, says Newman, the specific
and explicit arguments used but instead a person's ultimate
assumptions and expectations, which are normally not directly adverted to at all. The realization that differences between people in fact rest on positions and states of mind not
open to obvious view came early to Newman as one of his
deepest insights into the workings of the human mind. He
also saw very clearly that without "first principles" it would
be impossible to think at all. "Resolve to believe nothing,"
he wrote in 1841 in the *Tamworth Reading Room*, "and you
must prove your proofs and analyze your elements, sinking
further and further . . . till you come to the broad bosom of
scepticism. . . ."[3] Newman did not mean that we should not
examine our first principles, on which right thinking depends,
but he did hold that unless we assume something we shall not
be able to reason at all. This approach hardly tallied with the
confidence of nineteenth-century science in the possibility of
the straightforward attainment of truth in the area of factual

knowledge; but it seems to accord rather closely with the view of later twentieth-century philosophers of science that science develops on the basis of "hypotheses" which, having been tested rather than proved, appear best to account for the phenomena of scientific investigation, but which have never been actually demonstrated to be true.

In 1841[4] Newman also preached the last of a series of university sermons on faith and reason which he had begun in 1839. In the first of these ("Faith and Reason, Contrasted as Habits of Mind"), he starts by protesting against the popular idea that faith follows reason as a kind of "moral quality": or, in other words, that having made up our mind what to believe, we then "proceed to adore and to obey" ("Faith follows or not, according to the state of the heart"). On this view, faith ceases to be an intellectual act and becomes a kind of spiritual consequent of reasoning. But, Newman argues, just as a judge "does not make men honest, but acquits and vindicates them," so "Reason need not be the origin of Faith, as Faith exists in the very persons believing, though it does test and verify it."

Newman now makes the crucial distinction between "a critical" and "a creative power." We may, for example, give reasons for our actions by analyzing our motives, but the reasons are different from the motives. There is certainly no doubt that the New Testament sees "Faith . . . as an instrument of Knowledge and action, unknown to the world before . . . independent of what is commonly understood by Reason." If it were "merely . . . a believing upon evidence, or a sort of conclusion upon a process of reasoning," then it would scarcely be "a novel principle of action," as the Bible regards it. Just as conscience does not "depend . . . upon some previous processes of Reason" (although it is not "against Reason"), similarly "a child or uneducated person may . . . savingly act on Faith, without being able to produce reasons why he so acts." For faith is "mainly swayed by antecedent considerations," while reason calls for "direct and definite proof." Religious faith, Newman maintains, is, like all beliefs, "influenced

... less by evidence, more by previously-entertained principles, views, and wishes," in other words, by "antecedent probabilities." It is when these "prepossessions" are right, that "we are right in believing," albeit "upon slender evidence." Faith, then, is a "moral principle" in the sense that it is "created in the mind, not so much by facts, as by probabilities," which vary according to one's "moral temperament"—"A good man and a bad man will think very different things probable." This is why "a man *is* responsible for his faith, because he is responsible for his likings and dislikings, his hopes and his opinions, on all of which his faith depends." It is those "feelings"—which, Newman carefully adds, "come only of supernatural grace"—that "make us think evidence sufficient, which falls short of a proof in itself." And so it is that "religious minds embrace the Gospel mainly on the great antecedent probability of a Revelation, and the suitableness of the Gospel to their needs." However, not only are "Evidences ... thrown away" on "men of irreligious minds," but too much emphasis on them encourages people "to think that Faith is mainly the result of argument" and that "religious Truth is a legitimate matter of disputation" without any "preparation of heart": for "the ways towards Truth are considered high roads open to all men, however disposed, at all times," on the assumption that "Truth is to be approached without homage."

With that careful balance which we shall see is so characteristic of his theology, Newman proceeds to dismiss the other extreme, the "wild" anti-intellectual

> notion that actually no proof at all is implied in the maintenance, or may be exacted for the profession of Christianity. I would only maintain that that proof need not be the subject of analysis, or take a methodical form, or be complete and symmetrical, in the believing mind; and that probability is its life. I do but say that it is antecedent probability that gives meaning to those arguments from facts which are commonly called the Evidences of Revelation; that, whereas mere probability proves nothing, mere facts persuade no one; that probability is to fact,

as the soul to the body; that mere presumptions may have no force, but that mere facts have no warmth. A mutilated and defective evidence suffices for persuasion where the heart is alive; but dead evidences, however perfect, can but create a dead faith.

This brilliant sermon concludes with a well-known passage:

> Half the controversies in the world are verbal ones; and could they be brought to a plain issue, they would be brought to a prompt termination. Parties engaged in them would then perceive, either that in substance they agreed together, or that their difference was one of first principles. . . . We need not dispute, we need not prove,—we need but define. . . . Controversy, at least in this age, does not lie between the hosts of heaven, Michael and his Angels on the one side, and the powers of evil on the other; but it is a sort of night battle, where each fights for himself, and friend and foe stand together. When men understand each other's meaning, they see, for the most part, that controversy is either superfluous or hopeless.[5]

The stress on defining may remind us of Newman's insistence in *The Idea of a University* that "the philosophy of an imperial intellect . . . is based, not so much on simplification as on discrimination" and that its "true representative defines, rather than analyzes."[6] The point is surely very similar. There Newman was concerned with understanding how the different parts of knowledge fit together. Here he wants to emphasize the importance of understanding why people take up the positions they do rather than of proving or refuting the actual positions themselves. To understand what underlies a particular statement or point of view is for Newman to understand that statement or point of view, which in an important sense transcends the need actually to prove or refute it.

In the next sermon, "The Nature of Faith in Relation to Reason," Newman changes his strategy. Refusing now to accept the limited sense in which empiricists like Locke use the word *reason,* he effectively widens the terms of the debate by defining faith as "the reasoning of a religious mind, or of what

Scripture calls a right or renewed heart, which acts upon presumptions rather than evidence; which speculates and ventures on the future when it cannot make sure of it." If faith is regarded merely as "bad" reason, this is precisely "because it rests on presumption more, and on evidence less." There is no doubt that an act of faith is "an exercise of Reason," insofar as it is "an acceptance of things as real, which the senses do not convey, upon certain previous grounds." As such, it "is not the only exercise of Reason, which, when critically examined, would be called unreasonable, and yet is not so." The "pursuit of truth" is not exclusively "a syllogistic process," while "the experience of life contains abundant evidence that in practical matters, when their minds are really roused, men commonly are not bad reasoners," if only because "the principles which they profess guide them unerringly to their legitimate issues." Certainly people "may argue badly, but they reason well; that is, their professed grounds are no sufficient measures of their real ones," which "they do not, or cannot produce, or if they could, yet could not prove to be true, on latent or antecedent grounds which they take for granted." However "full" and "precise" the "grounds" and "however systematic our method, however clear and tangible our evidence, yet when our argument is traced down to its simple elements, there must ever be something assumed ultimately which is incapable of proof."

Faith, then, is not essentially different from other kinds of intellectual activity where "we must assume something to prove anything, and can gain nothing without a venture." In fact, the more important the knowledge is, the more subtle is "the evidence on which it is received," for "We are so constituted, that if we insist upon being as sure as is conceivable, in every step of our course, we must be content to creep along the ground, and can never soar." And so just as "Reason, with its great conclusions, is confessedly a higher instrument than Sense with its secure premises, so Faith rises above Reason, in its subject-matter, more than it falls below it in the obscurity of its process." Like "the most remarkable victories of genius," the act of faith involves "grounds of inference" which "cannot be exhibited," so that the "act of mind" of an uneducated believer "may be analogous to the exercise of sagacity in a great statesman or general, supernatural grace doing for the uncultivated reason what genius does for them."[7]

In "Love the Safeguard of Faith against Superstition," like the previous two sermons preached in 1839, Newman explains that the "antecedent probabilities" on which faith depends are "grounds which do not reach so far as to touch precisely the desired conclusion, though they tend towards it, and may come very near it." An "active," "personal and living" faith is created by "anticipations and presumptions," which "are the creation of the mind itself," and is an acceptance of an "external religion" which "elicits into shape, and supplies the spontaneous desires and presentiments of their minds." The "evidence" for Christianity "tells a certain way, yet might be more," and somebody will believe or not believe "according to . . . the state of his heart." Furthermore, "the antecedent judgment, with which a man approaches the subject of religion, not only acts as a bearing this way or that,—as causing him to go out to meet the evidence in a greater or less degree, and nothing more,—but, further, it practically colours the evidence." This is indeed how "judgments are commonly formed concerning facts alleged or reported in political and social matters, and for the same reason, because it cannot be helped."

Unbelief, for its part, "criticizes the evidence of Religion, only because it does not like it, and really goes upon presumptions and prejudices as much as Faith does, only presumptions of an opposite nature." Newman allows that "some safeguard of Faith is needed, some corrective principle which will secure it from running (as it were) to seed, and becoming superstition or fanaticism." What, therefore, "gives . . . birth" to faith is also what "disciplines it"—namely, "a right state of heart." In short, "We *believe*, because we *love*." Thus it is the "divinely-enlightened mind" which "sees in Christ the very Object whom it desires to love and worship,—the Object correlative of its own affections." There is, then, a moral as well as an intellectual element in faith:

> Right faith is the faith of a right mind. Faith is an intellectual act; right Faith is an intellectual act, done in a certain moral disposition. Faith is an act of Reason, viz. a reasoning upon presumptions; right Faith is a reasoning upon holy, devout, and enlightened presumptions. Faith ventures and hazards; right Faith ventures and hazards deliberately, seriously, soberly, piously, and humbly, counting the cost and delighting in the sacrifice.

Even though faith "is itself an intellectual act," still "it takes its character from the moral state of the agent" and "is perfected, not by intellectual cultivation, but by obedience."[8]

The eighteenth century, the "age of reason," had emphasized the "evidences" for Christianity. But unlike so many of his contemporaries in the nineteenth century, Newman did not react by adopting a "romantic" religion of feelings and imagination. Rather than opposing faith and reason, his achievement was to redefine faith in terms of a wider concept of reasoning than had been current since the seventeenth century. As in his educational theory, so in his philosophy he is concerned with the whole mind, not just the narrowly logical faculty. Similarly, he is also anxious to integrate the intellectual with the moral dimension.

But he remains insistent on the importance of the explicitly and specifically rational element, as the next sermon, "Implicit and Explicit Reason," preached in 1840, shows.

> Nothing would be more theoretical and unreal than to suppose that true Faith cannot exist except when moulded upon a Creed, and based upon Evidence; yet nothing would indicate a more shallow philosophy than to say that it ought carefully to be disjoined from dogmatic and argumentative statements. To assert the latter is to discard the science of theology from the service of Religion; to assert the former, is to maintain that every child, every peasant, must be a theologian. Faith cannot exist without grounds or without an object; but it does not follow that all who

have faith should recognize, and should be able to state what they believe, and why.

Scripture, Newman argues, makes it clear that faith is sometimes "attended by a conscious exercise of Reason," but sometimes is "independent not of objects or grounds (for that is impossible,) but of perceptible, recognized, producible objects and grounds." The difference between "the more simple faculties and operations of the mind, and that process of analyzing and describing them, which takes place upon reflection," is the difference between implicit and explicit reasoning. Newman's extraordinary sensitivity to and fascination with the workings of the mind is never more marvelously rendered than in this compelling and evocative passage:

> The mind ranges to and fro, and spreads out, and advances forward with a quickness which has become a proverb, and a subtlety and versatility which baffle investigation. It passes on from point to point, gaining one by some indication; another on a probability; then availing itself of an association; then falling back on some received law; next seizing on testimony; then committing itself to some popular impression, or some inward instinct, or some obscure memory; and thus it makes progress not unlike a clamberer on a steep cliff, who, by quick eye, prompt hand, and firm foot, ascends how he knows not himself, by personal endowments and by practice, rather than by rule, leaving no track behind him, and unable to teach another. It is not too much to say that the stepping by which great geniuses scale the mountains of truth is as unsafe and precarious to men in general, as the ascent of a skilful mountaineer up a literal crag. It is a way which they alone can take; and its justification lies in their success. And such mainly is the way in which all men, gifted or not gifted, commonly reason,—not by rule, but by an inward faculty.

After all, Newman insists, reasoning is "not an art," but "a living spontaneous energy within us," which the mind may afterwards "analyze" in its "various processes." Nobody can help reasoning, "but all men do not reflect upon their own reasonings, much less reflect truly and accurately, so as to do justice to their own meaning."

In other words, all men have a reason, but not all men can give a reason. We may denote, then, these two extremes of mind as reasoning and arguing, or as conscious and unconscious reasoning, or as Implicit Reason and Explicit Reasoning.

Newman points out that there are different kinds of reasoning appropriate to different kinds of subjects: "Some men's reason becomes genius in particular subjects, and is less than ordinary in others." A person may be very adept at analyzing another person's reasoning, and still be "as little creative of the reasoning itself which he analyzes, as a critic need possess the gift of writing poems." The corollary is that faith, "though in all cases a reasonable process, is not necessarily founded on investigation, argument, or proof; these processes being but the explicit form which the reasoning takes in the case of particular minds." But he points out that "No analysis is subtle and delicate enough to represent adequately the state of mind under which we believe, or the subjects of belief, as they are presented to our thoughts." It is only to be expected that apologists for Christianity should propose "as reasons for belief" those "secondary points" which "best admit of being exhibited in argument"—that is, the so-called "evidences"—as opposed to the "more recondite feelings" which are generally "the real reasons" for faith; for it is these latter "momentous reasons" which are not easily open to analysis and demonstration. Even the "evidences" usually convince only "upon a number of very minute circumstances together, which the mind is quite unable to count up and methodize in an argumentative form." He concludes on a note of caution: the "argumentative forms" which analyze or test reasoning are "critical, not creative," with the consequence that they are "useful in raising objections, and in ministering to scepticism." Indeed, there is always the danger of "weakening the springs of action by inquiring into them."[9]

The connection between Newman's philosophy of mind and his educational theory clearly emerges in the final sermon, "Wisdom, as Contrasted with Faith and with Bigotry," which was preached in 1841. Newman begins by differentiating between faith as "an exercise of the Reason, so spontaneous, unconscious, and unargumentative, as to seem at first sight even to be a moral act, and Wisdom being that orderly and mature development of thought, which in earthly language goes by the name of science and philosophy." This leads to a consideration of what Newman calls the "philosophical" mind. We hear that "knowledge itself, though a condition of the mind's enlargement, yet, whatever be its range, is not that very thing which enlarges it," but that "this enlargement consists in the comparison of the subjects of knowledge one with another." This view of the mind carries obvious implications for education:

> It is not the mere addition to our knowledge which is the enlargement, but the change of place, the movement onwards, of that moral centre, to which what we know and what we have been acquiring, the whole mass of our knowledge, as it were, gravitates. And therefore a philosophical cast of thought, or a comprehensive mind, or wisdom in conduct or philosophy, implies a connected view of the old with the new; an insight into the bearing and influence of each part upon every other; without which there is no whole, and could be no centre. It is the knowledge, not only of things, but of their mutual relations. It is organized, and therefore living knowledge.

A decade or so before he wrote the *Discourses*, Newman is already emphatic that "knowledge without system is not Philosophy," whereas "Philosophy is Reason exercised upon Knowledge," for "Reason is the power of proceeding to new ideas by means of given ones."

> It is the power of referring every thing to its true place in the universal system. . . . It makes every thing lead to every thing else; it communicates the image of the whole body to every

separate member, till the whole becomes in imagination like a spirit, every where pervading and penetrating its component parts, and giving them their one definite meaning.

There is already, too, the same marked element of hyperbole. Thus there is no possibility of the genuinely "philosophical" mind being "possessed by some one object," or, conversely, lacking a "firm grasp of principles" or a "view," since

> . . . Philosophy cannot be partial, cannot be exclusive, cannot be impetuous, cannot be surprised, cannot fear, cannot lose its balance, cannot be at a loss, cannot but be patient, collected, and majestically calm, because it discerns the whole in each part, the end in each beginning, the worth of each interruption, the measure of each delay, because it always knows where it is, and how its path lies from one point to another.[10]

These five sermons together constitute Newman's most significant and substantial contribution to the philosophy of religion prior to his *An Essay in Aid of a Grammar of Assent* (1870). Their originality lies, first of all, in their refusal to accept the received understanding of reason. Since the seventeenth century, philosophers had generally restricted reasoning either to Cartesian rationalism or Lockean empiricism: knowledge was either deduced from logical a priori truths or derived a posteriori from sense experience by induction, or from both. The kind of reasoning that Newman thinks leads to religious belief is not therefore "rational" reasoning at all. But if so, claims Newman, then neither is all that other reasoning, which is neither strictly logical nor empirical, but which we use and assume to be reliable and valid in all kinds of subject matters. There are all sorts of truths which we take for granted are true and yet which we cannot prove either by logic or by sense perception. And this is particularly true of the more important questions in life. The reasoning, therefore, that is involved in religious faith, far from being *sui generis*, is not different in kind from other reasoning of a nonlogical and nonempirical nature. Our ordinary beliefs,

such as, for example, that the sun will rise tomorrow or that
my wife loves me, are not susceptible of either deductive or
inductive *proof*, but we do not therefore think of them as
"unreasonable"—although from the perspective of the philosophy of the Enlightenment they are formally "irrational."
The great merit of the *Oxford University Sermons* is to show
that what is "irrational" from that philosophical point of view
which has so deeply colored and influenced our way of thinking (and still does) is not necessarily therefore "unreasonable."
What is "reasonable" is larger and wider than what is usually
suggested by the term *reason*.

Secondly, this type of reasoning depends not so much on
particular arguments and evidence as on existing assumptions
and expectations. The reason, Newman would say, why Ber-
trand Russell, for example, was an atheist was not that he had
proved by logic or established by scientific investigation that
Christianity was untrue, but rather that his attitude to life and
the world indicated or dictated that there was no need to
postulate a God. For Russell, to ask what ultimate meaning
life has, was itself, if not a meaningless question, certainly one
which there was no justification in asking. But, Newman
would add, while Russell's atheism was a natural or reasonable
result of his personal presumptions and principles, Russell's
own unbelief is just as unprovable and therefore (in Russell's
terms) irrational as the belief of Christians. For Newman there
could be no rigid separation of the man and the thinker:
Russell's thoughts on subjects outside formal logic are not
necessarily any more "logical," in the sense of "reasonable,"
than those of one untrained in philosophy. Nor could the
author of the *Idea of a University* allow that Russell's genius
in the field of formal logic gave him any automatic right to
be heard on subjects other than logic, that is to say, on such
subjects as are not susceptible to that particular type of reasoning.

The third important point Newman makes is that somebody may reason (in the larger, informal sense) perfectly well
but without being able to provide a rationale for his or her

thinking. Just as the creative writer is not necessarily the best
critic of his or her own writings, so we may have very good
reasons for thinking something and yet be incapable of analyzing or even producing those reasons. Newman has been accused of being an elitist because of his educational views and
because of his lack of views on social questions, but there is
nothing elitist, quite the contrary, about his defense of the
ordinary person's ability to reason correctly, which is based
on this crucial distinction between the thinking process itself
and the analysis or conscious awareness of that process. It is
true that uneducated persons may argue badly, but that does
not affect their capacity for reasoning. Newman's primary
concern may be to vindicate the ordinary, simple person's
right to religious belief, but the implications of his distinction
go much further. Newman was no advocate of political egali-
tarianism, but his conviction of the essential equality (at least
in principle) of people as reasoners makes him far more
"democratic" intellectually than most nineteenth-century
thinkers.

Fourthly, in the reasoning that pertains to religious belief
the moral element, far from being irrelevant, is seen as indispensable. It is because the good person has the right assumptions and expectations that he or she believes in God; whereas
the bad person will have equally good reasons for not believing
in God. The actual arguments that each will produce for their
beliefs or lack of beliefs can in the end be traced back to their
moral makeup. Newman does not mean that people may not
change or modify the first principles and antecedent probabilities they entertain, but he does mean that no amount of
argumentation can remove the fact that it is these which
determine the reasoning process that leads to belief or unbelief. And in the case of religious belief, Newman thought that
the "attempt to *see*" the relevant first principles, which are
necessarily of a moral nature, "by means of the intellect"
rather than by the conscience, was similar to the mistake of
"attempting by the intellect to see the physical facts" which
are perceived by the senses, which in turn "*enable* the intellect

to act, by giving it something to act upon."[11] The modern insistence on starting with the intellect in religious inquiry, he believed, was analogous to the medieval Schoolmen's use of syllogistic reasoning instead of empirical observation in scientific investigation.

Fifthly, Newman's developing epistemology is already clearly distinguished for the way in which it attempts to take account not just of the strictly deductive and inductive processes but also of other operations of the mind which were most often neglected by the philosophy of the Enlightenment. We have noted in particular the important part played by evaluative judgment in the formation of beliefs that are not founded in logical analysis or empirical observation. This is not to say that religious belief, for instance, should not be based on explicable arguments and grounds, but it is to say that believers may not know or be able to state clearly what they believe and why. For there is an important distinction between what Newman calls "explicit" and "implicit" reasoning. Moreover, there is no one single kind of reasoning, since it varies according to the subject matter: there are as many different kinds of reasoning as there are subjects to reason on. All this represents a much richer theory of knowledge than that which Newman found in the prevailing empiricist philosophy of his time.

Newman himself thought that the most "original" idea in the *Oxford University Sermons* was the argument that "antecedent probability is the great instrument of conviction in religious (nay in all) matters." He later wrote—in memorable words which again underline the "egalitarian" thrust of his epistemology—"It is how you convert factory girls as well as philosophers."[12] The emphasis on probability was an important element in the philosophy of Bishop Joseph Butler (1692–1752), whose classic work *The Analogy of Religion* (1736) had a deeply formative influence on Newman. The problem with this approach, which Newman later found in an amended version in John Keble's writings, was that it tended to undermine the whole idea of certainty. As he explained in the *Apologia*, Newman tried to "complete" the theory by arguing that "absolute certitude ... was the result of an *assemblage* of concurring and converging probabilities" and that "probabilities which did not reach to logical certainty, might suffice for a mental certitude; that the certitude thus brought about might equal in measure and strength the certitude which was created by the strictest scientific demonstration."[13]

So, for example, in the *Essay on the Development of Christian Doctrine* (1845) Newman talks of a "collection of weak evidences" which "makes up a strong evidence" and of "a converging evidence" which amounts to "proof." And without using the actual term *illative sense*, which does not appear before the *Grammar of Assent*, he also refers to the "prudence" or "prudent judgment" which decides when there is enough probability for conviction.[14] A year later, after his entry into the Roman Catholic Church, he insisted that "the measure of probability necessary for certainty" must vary "with the individual mind."[15] On the other hand, his subsequent stay in Rome (1846–47) and his contacts with Roman theologians made him very sensitive to the Church's insistence on "a rational faith ... built upon right reason." He therefore suggested that reasonable faith could "be the result of converging probabilities, and a cumulative proof" from "cumulating probabilities."[16] He continued to develop this position. The "proof of Religion," he wrote in a letter in 1861, using a striking analogy, "I liken ... to the mechanism of some triumph of skill ... where all display is carefully avoided, and the weight is ingeniously thrown in a variety of directions, upon supports which are distinct from, or independent of each other."[17] Or, as he later explained by an even more compelling analogy, "The best illustration ... is that of a *cable* which is made up of a number of separate threads, each feeble, yet together as sufficient as an iron rod," which "represents mathematical or strict demonstration."[18] The cable will certainly break if enough threads give way, but if the threads hold, then the cable is as strong as any metal bar. For, to use yet another image, a cumulation of probabilities is like a "bundle of sticks, each of which . . . you could snap in two, if taken separately from the rest."[19]

As well as considering the factors or process leading to conviction, Newman began to turn his thoughts to the nature of certainty itself. In a sermon of 1849, for instance, he wrote:

> Conviction is a state of mind, and it is something beyond and distinct from the mere arguments of which it is the result; it does not vary with their strength or their number. Arguments lead to a conclusion, and when the arguments are stronger, the conclusion is clearer; but conviction may be felt as strongly in consequence of a clear conclusion, as of one which is clearer.[20]

It is not, as he explains in a letter of the same year, "the mere perception of a conclusion, for then it would vary about with the strength of the premises."[21] The key distinction of the *Grammar of Assent* between assent and inference is not yet clearly formulated, but we can see Newman's mind moving in that direction. Certainly by 1853 the term *assent* is firmly established in his philosophical terminology: "Assent is the acceptance of a proposition as true." And the crucial difference between assent and inference is more clearly grasped: "Assent follows on inference, and that *by an act of the will.*" Newman is also clear that certainty, which is "an assent of the intellect to an assent," is a definite and fixed state of mind, for since "an assent does not admit of degrees, neither does certainty." But although he is insistent that there can be no degrees of assent, for "we cannot be more or less *certain* of a truth," still he does allow that "we can be certain of it with more vigour, keenness, and directness."[22]

The *Oxford University Sermons* had explored the nature of the reasoning involved in religious belief and had tried to show that this kind of reasoning, far from being peculiar to faith, is the very same type of informal reasoning that we employ without hesitation in many other areas of life, especially the ones that are most important to us. To this extent the analysis Newman offered constituted in itself a justification of the grounds of religious faith. But even if justifiable in terms of other kinds of similar intellectual acts, there was still the question of how far it is possible to achieve what may justifiably be called *certainty* in this kind of thinking and in what way such certainty differs from the certainty of the formal truths of logic and verifiable statements of fact. This was the central problem that was to shape Newman's philosophical thinking in the years ahead, until he worked out his final solution in the *Grammar of Assent*.

We can follow his progress as he noted down his thoughts in his philosophical notebook and in exploratory papers. By 1865 he had seen a parallel between what he now calls "certitude" and conscience, "which judges by a sort of instinct derived from moral practice, and reasons without scientific generalizations." One can no more live without conscience than "without some exercise of certitude." But like breathing, acts of certitude and conscience "are free and depend upon our will." Both certitude and conscience may turn out to be false, but there is no "test" to tell. However, the possibility of making a mistake is no excuse for not adhering to certitude and conscience. And Newman emphasizes that acts of certitude "generally succeed," and that even when they do not, they "are more consistent with our nature and our position in the world than a simple suspense of assent."[23]

Certitude is now clearly defined as "an assent deliberate, unconditional, and conscious, to a proposition as true." This does not mean that we cannot "allow that in the abstract it is possible that we are wrong." But there can be no "degrees" of certitude. The crucial distinction which Newman was to elaborate in the *Grammar* between assent and inference is implied in the comment that certitude, which is "already a full assent," "cannot be immediately dependent on the reasons which are its antecedents," unlike "conclusions," which "may be strengthened" by additional arguments. Further evidence, however, cannot make one more certain if one is already certain, but at the same time a cast-iron proof may not lead to assent, since assent is a personal act. Certitude, argues

Newman, "is not the passive admission of a conclusion as necessary, but the recognition of it as true"; nor does it "come under the reasoning faculty; but under the imagination," for it is the assent to "a fact in itself, as presented to me by my imagination." Moreover, the "assent of certitude" is seen as "complex" in that it is the assent to the truth of a proposition.[24]

This developing "personalist" philosophy included further thoughts on the actual act of reasoning. What Newman had called "implicit reasoning" in the Oxford University Sermons is now referred to as "natural inference." In 1859 he noted that truth may be intuited as "something perceived without reason or middle term." Furthermore, "I do not advance from one proposition to another, when I know . . . my existence from being conscious of my feeling but one and the same act of consciousness brings home to me that which afterwards at leisure I draw out into two propositions." This kind of reasoning is not a "process" because "the truth flashes at once," a "kind of intuition" in which one sees "the truth all of a heap, by one act" (like Newton, who saw a mathematical truth without being able to prove it).[25]

In 1859 Newman also worked out a more "personalistic" argument from conscience for the existence of God than that contained in this brief and impersonal allusion in the Oxford University Sermons: "Conscience implies a relation between the soul and a something exterior, and that, moreover, superior to itself."[26] The point is now fully personalized: on analysis the experience of conscience "involves the idea of a Father and Judge."[27] And Newman quotes from his novel Callista (1856) the passage where the heroine avers that the dictate of conscience is not "a mere law of my nature . . . it is the echo of a person speaking to me. . . . An echo implies a voice; a voice a speaker. That speaker I love and I fear."[28] Or, as he was to put it in a rather more existential way in the Apologia: "if I am asked why I believe in a God, I answer that it is because I believe in myself, for I feel it impossible to believe in my own existence . . . without believing also in the existence of Him, who lives as a . . . Being in my conscience."[29]

In 1860 he contemplated writing "a new work, [which] would be on 'the popular, practical, and personal evidence of Christianity—' i.e. as contrasted to the scientific, and its object would be to show that a given individual, high or low, has as much right (has as real rational grounds) to be certain, as a learned theologian who knows the scientific evidence."[30] It is true, of course, that Newman had important scriptural and theological reasons for vindicating the belief of the ordinary nonintellectual Christian. But his point has a much wider philosophical significance, since it involves a radical criticism of what conventionally passed for rationality.

During the succeeding years he continued to put down on paper his thoughts on certainty and certitude, but he was so distracted by other work as well as by the difficulty of the subject that there was still no sign of any book coming to fruition. In 1870, just before publication of the *Grammar of Assent*, he mentioned that he had been trying to write the book for the last thirty or forty years ever since his first university sermon on the question of faith in 1832. It was "like tunnelling through the Alps,"[31] he recalled—and in fact the breakthrough came in August 1866 when he was holidaying in the Swiss Alps: "At last, when I was up at Glion over the lake of Geneva, it struck me 'You are wrong in beginning with certitude—certitude is only a kind of assent—you should begin with contrasting assent and inference.'"[32] At last he had found "the point from which to begin." It was not that his "fundamental ideas" had not been "ever the same," but he had not been able to "carry them out." Now he had discovered "the clue, the 'Open Sesame,' of the whole subject."[33] He must begin with assent, not certitude.

Nearly all Newman's published writings were "occasional," that is to say, they were written for a particular occasion, often of a controversial nature. The *Grammar of Assent* is the one great exception: far from being written in the heat of the moment, it was in effect the work of a lifetime. Given the absence of any specific controversy and given his many vain attempts to write the book, the abrupt, dry beginning to the

Grammar is perhaps not so unexpected; as for the disconcerting lack of any introductory explanation, there survive several draft prefaces in which Newman betrays a rather nervous defensiveness, particularly with regard to his failure to follow the traditional Scholastic philosophy of the Roman Catholic Church, all of which, however, he discarded, deciding no doubt that it was more prudent to eschew apologies and explanations and plunge "in medias res," leaving it to readers to discover for themselves the true nature of the book.[34]

The *Grammar* is effectively divided into two distinct parts.[35] The first part is concerned with the relation between assent and apprehension, and attempts to show that it is justifiable to believe what one cannot wholly understand. The opening chapter begins by stating the fundamental distinction between assent, which is unconditional, and inference, which is conditional. Apprehension of the terms of a proposition is needed for assent, but not for inference. Apprehension is something less than understanding, since it is "simply an intelligent acceptance of the idea, or of the fact which a proposition enunciates."[36] "Notional" propositions, involving "common nouns . . . standing for what is abstract, general, and non-existing," require notional apprehension; whereas "real" propositions, "which are composed of singular nouns, and of which the terms stand for things external to us, unit and individual," require real apprehension. Newman makes the important reservation that a given proposition may have "a notional sense as used by one man, and a real as used by another"; words which are "a mere common-place," an "expression of abstractions" to one person, may bring "a lively image" before the imagination of another person. Real apprehension, then, is "stronger" in the sense of being "more vivid and forcible," since "intellectual ideas cannot compete in effectiveness with the experience of concrete facts."[37] The corollary is that assent is "stronger," though equally "unreserved," when the apprehension is of an "image" rather than an abstract truth, and therefore keener and more energetic.[38] The third chapter develops the critical distinction: "according as language expresses things external to us, or our own thoughts, so is apprehension real or notional."[39]

> The terms of a proposition do or do not stand for things. If they do, then they are singular terms, for all things that are, are units. But if they do not stand for things they must stand for notions, and are common terms. Singular nouns come from experience, common from abstraction. The apprehension of the former I call real, and of the latter notional.

Even past experiences of concrete things are susceptible of real apprehension through memory, which "consists in a present imagination of things that are past," which remain "things still, as being the reflections of things in a mental mirror." These impressions of past experiences include mental acts which are also "things," the images of which may be much more vivid than those of sensible objects. It may not always be easy to distinguish memory from abstraction, but whenever we have "images of things individual" we have real apprehension. What is true of memory is also true of imaginative creation, for we are able "to form, out of such passive impressions as experience has . . . left on our minds, new images, which, though mental creations, are in no sense abstractions, and though ideal, are not notional."[40]

Our experience, then, is of individual things, but our inevitable comparison of them means our "rising from particulars to generals, that is from images to notions."[41] We move away from the real apprehension of things in order to achieve breadth of mind and make progress in knowledge—even though real apprehension still "has the precedence, as being the scope and end and the test of notional." It is the "variation of vividness" in the two kinds of apprehension which accounts for apparent degrees in the act of assent, for as "notions come of abstractions" and "images come of experiences," "the more fully the mind is occupied by an experience, the keener will be its assent to it, if it assents, and on the other hand, the duller will be its assent and the less operative, the more it is engaged with an abstraction."[42] Notional assent can look very like inference, which is normally accompanied by notional apprehension just as assent is normally accompanied by real apprehension; whereas, "when inferences are exercised on things, they tend to be conjectures or presentiments, without logical force; and when assents are exercised on notions, they tend to be mere assertions without any personal hold on them on the part of those who make them."[43] This is why the clearer the inference, the less forcible the assent tends to be, and the more intense the assent, the less distinct the inference. While in notional assents "the mind contemplates its own creations instead of things," "in real, it is directed towards things, represented by the impressions which they have left on the imagination."[44] Of course, imagination may usurp reason and create assent where it is only intended to intensify it, so that "the distinctness of the images . . . is no warrant for the existence of the objects which those images represent."[45] Because real, unlike notional, assents are not common but personal and individual, they may be divisive and unreliable, but ultimately they are what give us our intellectual moorings, as well as stimulating us to action through the power of the imagination.

The first part of the *Grammar* concludes, like the second part, with an attempt to apply its conclusions to religious faith. A dogma is defined as a proposition which stands for either a notion and a truth or a thing and a reality: if the former, then the assent one gives will be a notional and theological assent of the intellect; if the latter, then the assent will be a real and religious assent of the imagination. Just as our knowledge of the external world is derived instinctively through and in the sense phenomena we experience, "so from the perceptive power which identifies the intimations of conscience with the reverberations or echoes . . . of an external admonition, we proceed on to the notion of a Supreme Ruler and Judge, and then again we image Him and His attributes in those recurring intimations, out of which, as mental phenomena, our recognition of His existence was originally gained." Conscience itself has two aspects—"it is a moral sense, and a sense of duty; a judgment of the reason and a magisterial dictate"; it "has both a critical and judicial office." It is in the latter aspect of a "sanction" rather than a "rule" of right conduct that conscience is primary, for it is as "a voice, or the echo of a voice, imperative and constraining," that conscience is unique in our experience. Newman admits that recognizing God "in the dictate of conscience" and "imaging the thought of Him in the definite impressions which conscience creates" would probably be impossible without some "extrinsic help." Our image of God is clarified through revelation and deepened through devotion. It is possible to assent to a personal God either as a theological truth or as a religious reality. But a dogmatic creed, far from being alien to a living, personal faith, is necessary because there is a need for facts to be expressed in language and for the exposition of "the truths on which the religious imagination has to rest"; likewise, because "knowledge must ever precede the exercise of the affections," religion cannot do without theology. Thus our apprehension of, and assent to, the Trinity as a complex whole or mystery is notional, because "though we can image the separate propositions, we cannot image them altogether."[46] As for the many dogmatic propositions to which a Catholic is required to give notional assent, his assent is implicitly given when he gives a real assent to the Church.

Before proceeding to the second half of the *Grammar*, it is important to clarify the fundamental distinction between notional and real apprehension and assent. First of all, it is worth noting that it would be wrong to try and erect any division between the terms of the proposition in question and its actual apprehension, for "we cannot draw the line between the object and the act . . . as is the thing apprehended, so is the apprehension."[47] What is in question is not the subjective apprehension of the objective proposition, but the sense of the proposition as used by different people or by the same person in two different ways. For Newman there could be no separation of the meaning from the use of a proposition.

On the other hand, Newman has been criticized for making

too rigid a distinction of kind between the notional and the real, when in fact there is only a distinction of degree. Thus it has been objected that by saying that sight is the most vivid kind of sense experience, Newman seems to be saying that people who lack visual imagery are incapable of real apprehension and assent. This would appear to imply that one person's visual image of an event he has never seen cannot be more vivid than that of another person who has seen it, when this is manifestly not the case. But in fact real apprehension and assent, far from being necessarily tied to the visual sense, are not even bound up with sense experience at all. The confusion seems to arise from Newman's saying that real propositions are "more vivid and forcible" because "intellectual ideas cannot compete in effectiveness with the experience of concrete facts."[48] This, not unnaturally, has misled critics into thinking that real assent is concerned only with concrete propositions, and notional with abstract, whereas it is clear that people can be far more excited by intellectual ideas than by the most physical of experiences. But Newman does not deny this. At the very beginning of the book he points out that "a mere common-place, a terse expression of abstractions" may be "the record of experiences, a sovereign dogma, a grand aspiration, inflaming the imagination, piercing the heart." In other words, it may indeed be the object of a real assent. For in this case the general idea becomes "a living image"—though there is no mental image of a visual or sensory kind.[49] In fact, Newman states categorically that an apprehension of a definite mental act is an apprehension of a "thing" (as opposed to "notion"), conceivably with "an individuality and completeness which outlives the impressions made by sensible objects." Similarly, it is possible out of the "passive impressions" of experience to form images "which, though mental creations, are in no sense abstractions, and though ideal, are not notional."[50] What makes propositions concrete and enables assent to be real is "experience" and the element of the "personal."[51]

If, then, we take something as notional as Newman's be-

loved "first principles," which are "notions, not images, because they express what is abstract, not what is individual and
from direct experience," these may elicit a *real* assent "when
we apply our general knowledge to a particular instance of
that knowledge," for "these so-called first principles . . . are
really conclusions or abstractions from particular experiences;
and an assent to their existence is not an assent to things or
their images, but to notions, real assent being confined to the
propositions directly embodying these experiences." Such is
the difference between knowing "the received rules" of a profession and entering into them in practice, between "intellectually recognizing" a truth and seeing or feeling it, between
"accepting a notion" and "realizing a fact." Even so abstract a
principle as "the inviolability of the laws of nature" may become a "vivid impression," a "distinct and eloquent" image,
to a philosopher of the school of Hume. Assents "as given to
moral objects . . . are perhaps as real as they are powerful,"
and "till we have them, in spite of a full apprehension and
assent in the field of notions, we have no intellectual moorings. . . . These beliefs . . . form the mind out of which they
grow."[52] Indeed, for Newman the most important real assent
a person is capable of is to the existence of God—and here
there is nothing remotely "concrete" in the usual sense of the
word. For it is conscience which "provides for the mind a real
image of God," an image which is in no way sensory, but
which is experienced and vivid.[53] The whole theory of real
assent demands that there should be notional concepts so
vividly realized as to become facts in the imagination, that is,
in Newman's terminology, images.

The second part of the *Grammar* is almost a different book,
although of course it depends on the theory of assent developed in the first half. At last Newman turns to his central
concern: how is one justified in believing what one cannot
prove? He begins by returning to his initial distinction between assent and inference. The problem is whether, given
that nonlogical reasoning never rises above probability (as
opposed to logical certainty), the assent in such cases also

varies in degree according to the strength of the probability. In formal logical propositions the unconditional assent merely satisfies logically necessary conclusions. But in practice we find there are "many truths in concrete matter, which no one can demonstrate, yet every one unconditionally accepts."[54] Far from being merely the conclusion without the premises to an inference, assent does not depend upon the inference any more than the strongest inference necessarily elicits assent. In the case of logical truths, assent immediately follows on the demonstration, because "the correlative of ascertained truth is unreserved assent"[55]—although the assent is still distinct from the inference. A mathematician, for instance, may not assent to the conclusion of his own proof until he has the support of another judgment besides his own. However, just as there are no degrees of truth, so there are no degrees of assent. Suspicion and conjecture, for example, are unconditional assents to the probability of a proposition. A "half-assent"[56] is not an assent at all, but only an inclination to assent. The argument that assent to nonlogical truths must be conditional arises from a confusion between the act of assenting to a conclusion and the relation between the conclusion and its premises, for assent is related to a conclusion as sensation of cold or heat is related to the reading of the thermometer in the room. There are apparent exceptions: assent upon the authority of others is often not a true assent at all; "a *prima facie* assent is an assent to an antecedent probability of a fact, not to the fact itself"; a "conditional"[57] assent means an assent only under certain circumstances; a deliberate or slow assent refers to the circumstance of the assenting; an uncertain assent is an assent which may be given up because it is not habitual; a strong assent refers to the emotional concomitants of the assent; a luminous assent is an assent where the arguments in its favor are numerous and strong.

Newman now differentiates "simple" assent, which is unconscious, from "complex" or "reflex" assent, which is conscious and deliberate.[58] It is not investigation as such but inquiry which is incompatible with assent. It is true that an investigation may lead to a loss of assent, but the sense of the possibility of this loss is not the same as doubt—nor does assent imply an intention never to change one's mind, but, instead, the absence of any idea of ever changing. Assent to an assent is "certitude," the proposition is a "certainty," and the assenting is "knowing."[59] False certitudes are less common than is supposed. Certitude implies the confidence that even if certitude were to fail the certainty would remain, a requirement which disqualifies many so-called certitudes. There are various emotional signs which indicate a lack of real certitude, whereas a feeling of intellectual security signifies real certitude.

Newman at last arrives at the climax of the *Grammar*, the justification of religious certitude. He begins with the assent of faith, which, while unquestioning, is absolutely firm. Some assents of this kind may be lost in the process of trying to turn them into certitudes. The reflex assent of certitude is always notional because it is an assent to the truth of the simple assent. Just as the freshness and vigor of the original assent may be lost in the gaining of certitude, so too the argumentation prior to certitude may disturb the normal thought processes, encouraging doubt and reducing imaginative realities to notions. Certitude may not always be characterized by calm serenity, because of some unexpected surprise or temptation to doubt. The "human mind is made for truth,"[60] and so certitude includes the idea of indefectibility: the failure of certitude is the exception. But the fact is that there is no test for distinguishing true from false certitudes. Unlike infallibility, certitude is not a gift or a faculty, but a disposition of mind relative to a particular case. Thus one can be certain (but not infallible) about the infallibility of the Church. If certitude is unfounded, then it is the prior reasoning, not the actual assent, that is at fault, since to have refused assent in the face of a conclusion would have been to act against one's nature. The intellect may not be infallible, but it is capable of being certain. For example, one must be entitled to be certain that after all one has made a mistake in being certain about something. False certitudes are faults, not because they are certitudes, but because they are false:

> The sense of certitude may be called the bell of the intellect; and that it strikes when it should not is a proof that the clock is out of order, no proof that the bell will be untrustworthy and useless, when it comes to us adjusted and regulated. . . . conscience too may be said to strike the hours, and will strike them wrongly, unless it be duly regulated for the performance of its proper function.[61]

Not all so-called certitudes, however, are true certitudes, which should only follow after examination and proof, as well as being restricted to certain occasions and subject matter. Opinion is far more attainable than certitude, but even probability presupposes the certainty of first principles. An acceptance of a religious faith involves different kinds of assents, but a change of religion may merely mean the realization and development of one or more basic and continuing certitudes. It would be quibbling to say that certitude is a conviction of what is true and that a false certitude is not a certitude at all. But it is generally true that indefectibility is a negative test of certitude: to lose one's conviction is to show that one never had certitude, because certitude is impregnable against all shocks.

The discussion now turns to the question of how in fact certitude is normally attained. Newman begins by contrasting informal reasoning with formal inference, of which the most logical form is the syllogism. The perfection of strictly logical reasoning lies in the fact that words which denote things and which have innumerable implications are stripped of their concrete meanings precisely in order to be abstract and notional. But the abstract cannot reach the concrete. Logical inference cannot produce proof in concrete matters because its premises are assumed and ultimately depend upon first principles, wherein lies the real problem of attaining to truth. For logic cannot prove the first principles which it assumes.

Abstract arguments reach probability but not certainty in concrete matters, because they do not touch the particular. The language of logic has its obvious advantages in the pursuit of knowledge, but human thought is too personal and complex to "admit of the trammels of any language."[62]

We have now reached the heart of the book. It is in fact, Newman argues, the cumulation of probabilities, which cannot be reduced to a syllogism, that leads to certainty in the concrete. Many certitudes depend on informal proofs, whose reasoning is more or less implicit. As we view the objects of sense, so we grasp the proof of a concrete truth as a whole "by a sort of instinctive perception of the legitimate conclusion in and through the premises."[63] Such implicit reasoning is too personal for logic. The rays of truth stream through the medium of our moral as well as our intellectual being. As we gain a perspective of a landscape, so we personally grasp a truth with a "real ratiocination and present imagination" which reaches beyond the "methodical process of inference." Such "supra-logical judgment" is an "individual perception" under the influence of "an intellectual conscientiousness."[64] In religion, the "moral state" of the inquirer is also very important. But otherwise, in all subjects "the principle of concrete reasoning is parallel to the method of proof which is the foundation of modern mathematical science," in which the conclusion "is foreseen and predicted rather than actually attained; foreseen in the number and direction of accumulated premises, which all converge to it . . . yet do not touch it logically . . . on account of the nature of its subject-matter, and the delicate and implicit character of at least part of the reasonings on which it depends."[65] And so the mind in concret matters progresses from probable antecedents to sufficient proof, and finally to certitude.

"Natural" inference, or the implicit, unconscious, and instinctive movement from antecedent to consequent, proceeds not from propositions to propositions, but from concrete things to concrete things, without conscious recognition of the antecedent or the process of inference. This is in fact our natural way of reasoning, employed both by the peasant and the genius; it is an instinctive perception, although not a natural instinct, which is one and the same in all. It may be damaged by learning rules or resorting to artificial aids. Like our taste, our reasoning is spontaneous and unselfconscious. It varies according to the subject matter and has many different forms. "Judgment then in all concrete matters is the architectonic faculty; and what may be called the Illative Sense, or right judgment in ratiocination, is one branch of it."[66]

Newman insists that his purpose is not metaphysical, like that of the idealists who defend the certainty of knowledge against skeptical empiricists, but is "of a practical character, such as that of Butler in his *Analogy,*" namely, to ascertain the nature of inference and assent. Certitude, it has been shown, is "an active recognition of propositions as true" in response to a proof. And "the sole and final judgment on the validity of an inference in concrete matter is committed to the personal action of the ratiocinative faculty, the perfection or virtue of which I have called the Illative Sense, a use of the word 'sense' parallel to our use of it in 'good sense.'"[67] We have to accept our nature as it is, for it is "a fact not admitting of question, all things being of necessity referred to it, not it to other things": "I cannot think . . . about my being, without starting from the very point which I aim at concluding."[68] Certainly, "there is no ultimate test of truth besides the testimony born to truth by the mind itself."[69] Thought is always thought, but it varies according to the subject matter, and there is no "ultimate test of truth and error" apart from the illative sense.[70] The mind outstrips language, contemplating first principles without words or any process of analysis, with the illative sense determining the beginning, the middle, and the end of any investigation.

Like the first part, the second part too ends with an attempt to apply its conclusions specifically to religious faith. Christianity may be "demonstrably true," but it is not "true irresistibly," because truth, like light, cannot be seen by the blind. Where assumptions are needed, Newman prefers to "attempt to prove Christianity in the same informal way in which I can prove for certain that I have been born."[71] First principles are all-important, and here "belief in revealed truths depends on belief in natural."[72] Acceptance of the arguments for Christianity rests on acceptance of certain general religious truths. The Christian revelation is "the completion and supplement of Natural Religion, and of previous revelations."[73]

Various objections have been made to different parts of the argument. First, the difference between assenting and inferring has not always been clearly grasped. Newman intends a logical distinction between two different kinds of act and the linguistic forms of propositions expressing them. It is not, for example, the difference between recognizing reasons for assenting and actually assenting. "Conditional" propositions express conclusions and imply a dependence on other propositions; whereas "categorical" propositions simply assert without any such implication. A conclusion is as distinct from an assertion "as a word of command is from a persuasion or recommendation."[74] Even where the conclusion of an argument is crystal clear, "assent would not in consequence be the same act as inference," although "it would certainly follow immediately upon it."

> I allow then as much as this, that, when an argument is in itself and by itself conclusive of a truth, it has by a law of our nature the same command over our assent, or rather the truth which it has reached has the same command, as our senses have. Certainly our intellectual nature is under laws, and the correlative of ascertained truth is unreserved assent.[75]

In other words, however inevitably assertion may follow conclusion, there are different kinds of intellectual and verbal acts involved in assent and inference. And this difference is embodied in the difference between unconditional and conditional propositions: "Inference is always inference; even if demonstrative, it is still conditional; it establishes an incontrovertible conclusion on the condition of incontrovertible premises. To the conclusion thus drawn, assent gives its absolute recognition."[76] It is wrong, then, to see the choice as between conditional inference characterized by reservations, on the one hand, and confident, undoubting assent on the other. For, while it is true that there can be no "variation of an assent to an inference," there are "assents to a variation in inferences." It is, in other words, possible to be "certain of an uncertainty."[77] Again, while it is true that "inference is ordinarily the antecedent of assent," that does not interfere with "the unconditional character of the assent, viewed in itself."[78]

Second, the intellectual character of the illative sense has not always been fully appreciated. Defined as "right judgment in ratiocination,"[79] the elements both of evaluating and reasoning need to be emphasized. In "informal reasoning," a man comes to a conclusion which is supported but not demonstrated by the evidence and for which he is "responsible to himself."[80] "Just as," Newman argues, "there is no sufficient test of poetical excellence, heroic action, or gentleman-like conduct, other than the particular mental sense, be it genius, taste, sense of propriety, or the moral sense, to which those subject-matters are severally committed," so "in no class of concrete reasonings, whether in experimental science, historical research, or theology, is there any ultimate test of truth and error in our inferences besides the trustworthiness of the Illative Sense that gives them its sanction."[81] The use of the word *sense*, then, is justified by the need to emphasize the "element of the personal" in the "living intellect," for our conclusions in informal reasoning are judgments arrived at by "the action of our own minds, by our own individual perception of the truth in question, under a sense of duty to those conclusions and with an intellectual conscientiousness."[82]

Third, Newman's theory of probability has been insufficiently understood. It has nothing to do with any kind of mechanical procedure for counting probabilities in some sort of numerical scale, for "a cumulation of probabilities, over and above their implicit character, will vary both in their number and their separate estimated value, according to the particular intellect which is employed upon it."[83] And so "proof" in concrete reasoning will always have an "element of the personal, because 'prudence' is not a constituent part of our nature, but a personal endowment."[84] Ordinary reasoning is carried out by "dealing with things directly . . . in the concrete, with an intrinsic and personal power, not a conscious adoption of an artificial instrument or expedient.[85] Newman also makes it quite clear that the cumulative argument from probability will vary in kind and method according to the nature of the subject matter. Thus, for example, we prove that Great Britain is an island in a very different kind of way from that by which we prove that one day I shall die.

Fourth, and most often voiced ever since the first reviews, is the objection to the claim that certitude is indefectible. Now it is perfectly true that Newman says that certitude "carries with it an inward assurance . . . that it shall never fail." But this confidence only reflects a general rule to which exceptions are always possible; Newman's concern, in his own words, is merely "to show, that, as a general rule, certitude does not fail." He qualifies this "inward assurance" by adding: "Indefectibility almost enters into its very idea, enters into it at least so far as this, that its failure, if of frequent occurrence, would prove that certitude was after all and in fact an impossible act." Actually, he argues, "failures of what was taken for certitude are the exception."[86] However, even though the possibility of error is freely admitted, still, "if we are never to be certain, after having been once certain wrongly, then we ought never to attempt a proof because we have once made a bad one." And indeed, error itself presupposes certitude, because if "I have been mistaken in my certitude, may I not at least be certain that I have been mistaken?"[87] But the fact remains that for Newman false certitudes are conceivable "in many cases," even as "false consciences abound."[88] Nevertheless, he holds to the general principle: "Premising that all rules are but general, especially those which relate to the mind, I observe that indefectibility may at least serve as a negative test of certitude, or *sine qua non* condition, so that whoever loses his conviction on a given point is thereby proved not to have been certain of it."[89] That the rule is only a general one is clear from what he says concerning changes of religious belief: "I will not urge ... that certitude is a conviction of what is true, and that these so called certitudes have come to nought, because, their objects being errors, not truths, they really were not certitudes at all."[90] And even after pointing to cases where ostensible certitude in religion transpires to be something less, Newman does not hesitate to admit: "All concrete laws are general, and persons, as such, do not fall under laws. Still, I have gone a good way, as I think, to remove the objections to the doctrine of the indefectibility of certitude in matters of religion, though I cannot assign to it an infallible token."[91] In other words, while the indefectibility of religious certitude is generally sustained, there is no absolute guarantee that it will not fail, for the simple reason that there are no absolute tests of true and false certainty.

The *Grammar*, then, does not purport to be a "metaphysical" work. Nor is it so much a "psychological" study as what we should now call a "phenomenological" analysis of that state of mind which we call certitude or certainty and of the cognitive acts involved in it. Religious certainty is seen as one of many kinds of certainty which are not proved either empirically or logically. The justification of religious belief merges into a much larger justification of the validity of various trains of thought which culminate in conviction. What, then, are we to say in conclusion of the *Grammar*'s philosophical insights?

First of all, the famous notional/real distinction, which is at the heart of Newman's phenomenology, stems from a philosophy of the mind which takes account not only of the logical or ratiocinative intellect but also of the imagination. Indeed, Newman had originally talked of "imaginative" as opposed to "real" apprehension and assent, nor did he completely abandon the usage in the *Grammar*. It appears from an earlier draft or paper that the main reason why he changed his terminology was to avoid any confusion with the

Coleridgean idea of the imagination as the "inventive power," which Newman regarded as a development or elaboration of the simpler sense of imagination, with which he was principally concerned.[92] But even if Newman wanted to keep a certain distance from Coleridge's theory, nevertheless the stress on the importance of the imagination for cognition is a crucial part of his strategy in redefining and enlarging—or perhaps rather restoring—our understanding of human intelligence. However, while the stress on imagination suggests an affinity with Coleridge and the influence of romanticism, the category of the "real," on the other hand, belongs to Newman's pragmatic realism. The role played by the imagination in apprehension and assent reminds us that Newman was deeply influenced by that very empiricism from which he was trying to escape. After all, the purpose of "images," we are told, is to bring concrete "things," as opposed to abstract notions, before our minds. The imagination enables us to see "things external to us" with the mind's eye, as opposed to thinking "our own thoughts" with the intellect. In other words, Newman's imagination, far from being introspective or detached from reality, leads us not into an inner world but into the outer world. Although, then, the theory of the "real" involves a wider concept of the human mind than that assumed by empiricism, nevertheless what enables apprehension and assent to be real is precisely the empirical factor of "experience."

The other element, as we have seen, which makes our apprehensions and assents real is the "personal" element. And this raises the second characteristic of Newman's philosophy, which is deeply "personalist" in a way that reminds one of Kierkegaard and existentialism. In place of the traditional arguments for the existence of God, Newman, as we have seen, prefers to personalize the issue, first by pointing to the uniqueness of conscience as a fact of our experience, and then by appealing to our own personal recognition of God "in the dictate of conscience." All this was very far from the usual arguments from the objective "evidences." But then Newman held that human thinking is a preeminently personal activity: I can only think my own thoughts; I cannot think the thoughts of another person. This is why thought cannot be reduced to any set linguistic form or logical syllogism. Truth has to be personally grasped; it cannot be imposed on us. We have to use our own "judgment," which is an "individual perception," and this in turn involves "an intellectual conscientiousness," which is again our own personal responsibility. Far from truth being passively accepted, certitude is "an active recognition of propositions as true," and "the sole and final judgment" we have to use in inference "is committed to the personal action" of the reasoning faculty. For indeed "there is no ultimate test of truth besides the testimony born to truth by the mind itself." Again, the force of the argument from "a cumulation of probabilities" depends on the "particular intellect," so that "proof" in concrete reasoning will always have an "element of the personal, because 'prudence' is not a constituent part of our nature, but a personal endowment."

Thirdly, Newman's treatment of doubt anticipates Wittgenstein's fundamental insight into the absurdity of universal skepticism, since to doubt everything is to nullify the language of doubt itself.[93] The only reason we can use the word *doubt* at all is because the word belongs to a language which also contains the idea of conviction. The possibility of error assumes the possibility of certainty: "may I not at least be certain that I have been mistaken?" Long before Wittgenstein, Newman saw clearly that one cannot stand outside or escape from the human mind and its thought and language. There is no alternative rationality, apart from the rationality we know and by means of which we know, to which we can appeal whether to justify or invalidate our thoughts. A radical skepticism is not only unnatural but meaningless. To show Newman's anticipation of Wittgenstein's radical critique of skeptical empiricism, the following passage (already glanced at) deserves to be quoted at length:

[it is] unmeaning in us to criticize or find fault with our own nature, which is nothing else than we ourselves, instead of using it according to the use of which it ordinarily admits. Our being, with its faculties, mind and body, is a fact not admitting of question, all things being of necessity referred to it, not it to other things.

. . . There is no medium between using my faculties, as I have them, and flinging myself upon the external world according to the random impulse of the moment, as spray upon the surface of the waves, and simply forgetting that I am.

I am what I am, or I am nothing. I cannot think, reflect, or judge about my being, without starting from the very point which I aim at concluding. My ideas are all assumptions, and I am ever moving in a circle. I cannot avoid being sufficient for myself, for I cannot make myself anything else, and to change me is to destroy me. If I do not use myself, I have no other self to use.[94]

As he noted succinctly in his philosophical notebook, "We must take ourselves for what we are—we cannot divide between the mind and its gifts—we only know the mind *through* its gifts and powers."[95]

The penetration of such writing indicates how Newman's achievement as a philosopher of religion is inseparable from the originality of his theory of knowledge. The importance, therefore, of his philosophical writings extends beyond the philosophy of religion into epistemology, and consequently touches on other areas of philosophical thought. The conventional view of Newman as an apologist for Christianity rather than, strictly speaking, a philosopher, needs to be seriously revised. Thus, for example, Frederick Copleston in his *A History of Philosophy* contends that it would be "misleading to describe *The Grammar of Assent* as a philosophical work," although (significantly) he allows that its "arguments are placed in a general logical and epistemological context."[96] It is time that more attention was paid to this "context," which has been too long ignored by philosophers, both of the Scholastic and empiricist traditions, but which ought to be of interest in a contemporary philosophical milieu where existentialist or phenomenological or Wittgensteinian ideas are current. The time seems ripe for a reappraisal of Newman's philosophical significance.

3

THE PREACHER

NEWMAN MAY HAVE THOUGHT that teaching was his real vocation and that his principal intellectual mission was the philosophical defense of religious belief, but the fact is that during at least the Anglican half of his life, he probably spent more time composing sermons than writing anything else. The eight volumes of *Parochial and Plain Sermons* (not to mention *Sermons Bearing on Subjects of the Day*) account for nearly a quarter of the thirty-six volumes in the collected uniform edition of the works. And these represent only about a third of the pastoral sermons he actually wrote as an Anglican. There are also, of course, a further two volumes of sermons which he published as a Catholic—*Discourses Addressed to Mixed Congregations* and *Sermons Preached on Various Occasions*. The former were formal compositions delivered in the first few years after his ordination in Rome, and they tend to be ornate and rhetorical in an Italianate manner; the latter again were not pastoral homilies but set pieces for special events. A small volume of posthumously published sermons (*Catholic Sermons of Cardinal Newman*) consists of some popular parochial sermons which he preached in his first year as a Catholic priest at St. Chad's, Birmingham. After he had read out the second one he gave up the Anglican practice of reading sermons. The record of his congregational preaching on Sundays at the Birmingham Oratory survives only in the form of the notes he took into the pulpit, which again have been

74

posthumously published (as *Sermon Notes of John Henry Cardinal Newman, 1849–1878*).

It is almost as hard to imagine the Oxford Movement without Newman's preaching in the university church of St. Mary's as without the *Tracts for the Times*. At this time of his life it was as a preacher that Newman was best known to his contemporaries, and even for a public that bought volumes of sermons as eagerly as the Victorians, his *Parochial and Plain Sermons* achieved remarkable sales. His Anglican sermons, at least, continue to be widely read, not only for their literary merits, but also, more importantly, because they constitute one of the undoubted classics of Christian spirituality.

The most famous description of Newman's legendary preaching is Matthew Arnold's romantic evocation of "the charm of that spiritual apparition, gliding in the dim afternoon light through the aisles of St. Mary's, rising into the pulpit, and then, in the most entrancing of voices, breaking the silence with words and thoughts which were a religious music,—subtle, sweet, mournful." It was the "sweetness" of this "musical" voice, low and soft but also "piercing" and "thrilling," which aroused most comment. The contrasted modulation of the speaking voice was the most notable characteristic of Newman's performance as a preacher, for his manner lacked all the usual accompaniments of pulpit oratory. The only oratorical device that Newman used was the long pause, but even that seemed to be not for effect but the result of sheer intensity of thought. What was also so striking about the more eloquent passages in the sermons was that they gave the impression of being the involuntary outpourings of a preacher unable to contain himself any longer, but only concerned to convey the most practical and real of messages in as plain and simple words as possible. The sermons were read, with hardly any change in the inflection of the voice and without any visible gesture on the part of the preacher, whose eyes remained fixed on the text in front of him.[1]

The preacher's appearance and voice may have seemed ethereal to his listeners, but what also struck them—and what still strikes a modern reader—was the stark, even harsh, realism of his words.[2] It is true that Newman as a Tractarian stressed the mystical, supernatural nature of Christianity, but there is nothing faintly mysterious about the obligations that he laid down as incumbent on the believer. He saw the vocation of the Christian as a simple one—"Be you content with nothing short of perfection." And he was unequivocal and unremitting in his demands on his congregation:

> We dwell in the full light of the Gospel, and the full grace of the Sacraments. We ought to have the holiness of Apostles. There is no reason except our own wilful corruption, that we are not by this time walking in the steps of St. Paul or St. John, and following them as they followed Christ.[3]

He could, of course, when he chose use all his rhetorical art to inspire his listeners with the ideal:

> Let us not be content with ourselves; let us not make our own hearts our home, or this world our home, or our friends our home; let us look out for a better country, that is, a heavenly. . . .
> Blessed are they who give the flower of their days, and their strength of soul and body to Him; blessed are they who in their youth turn to Him who gave His life for them, and would fain give it to them and implant it in them, that they may live for ever. Blessed are they who resolve—come good, come evil, come sunshine, come tempest, come honour, come dishonour—that He shall be their Lord and Master, their King and God! They will come to a perfect end, and to peace at the last.[4]

But, by contrast, the means to attaining the ideal are highly practical and specific. Newman's sermons are distinguished not for vague platitudes and pious aspirations, but for their utter concreteness and definiteness. If the ideals are high, even apparently unattainable, the spirituality is ruthlessly real, with no time for merely idealistic emotions or flourishes. The real Christian is characterized by his or her unpretentiousness. Heroism lies not in aiming at great deeds or sacrifices but in accepting daily ordinary mortifications. Thus "the self-denial which is pleasing to Christ consists in little things ... in the continual practice of small duties which are distasteful to us." He warned his congregation not to be "content with a warmth of faith carrying you over many obstacles," but to practice "daily self-denial" in "those little things in which obedience *is* a self-denial."[5] There is the typically realistic reminder that

> Nothing is more difficult than to be disciplined and regular in our religion. It is very easy to be religious by fits and starts, and to keep up our feelings by artificial stimulants; but regularity seems to trammel us, and we become impatient.[6]

Real holiness is attained by concrete acts of no particular significance in themselves, for we should remember "how mysteriously little things are in this world connected with great; how single moments, improved or wasted, are the salvation or ruin of all-important interests."[7] The hallmark of the truly spiritual person is that he or she "is *consistent*" in a "jealous carefulness about all things, little and great."[8] One day as a Catholic he would say, "I have ever made consistency the mark of a Saint," the greatest mortification being "to do well the ordinary duties of the day."[9] As an Anglican, he preached that real self-denial lies not in "literally bearing Christ's Cross, and living on locusts and wild honey, but in such light abstinences as come in our way."[10]

Far from assuming that Christians want to be holy, the sermons start from the eminently realistic assumption that the reason people sin is that they want to. It is not just that it is unrealistic to expect sudden transformations, and that if there is to be change there has to be the will to change, but this willingness is itself something that only gradually develops: "Is not holiness the result of many patient, repeated efforts after obedience, gradually working on us, and first modifying and then changing our hearts?"[11] Prayer itself has to be realistic:

it is quite unreal to pray to be good when one does not in fact particularly want to be good, and when it is in fact this desire to be good for which one should be praying. A shrewdly practical psychology informs the idealistic spirituality. Thus, for example, voluntary acts of self-denial are recommended as a means to acquiring self-control in order to guard against unexpected temptations like anger, which "are irresistible perhaps when they come upon you, but it is only at times that you are provoked, and then you are off your guard; so that the occasion is over, and you have failed, before you were well aware of its coming."[12]

False illusions about self are mercilessly exposed. A man's real "trial," for instance, lies in his "weak point," and "not in those things which are easy to him, but in that one thing, in those several things, whatever they are, in which to do his duty is against his nature."[13] "Any one deliberate habit of sin," Newman warns severely, "incapacitates a man for receiving the gifts of the Gospel."[14] A total commitment to Christ, he remarks, is "rare," for most Christians retain "a reserve" in their obedience, a "corner" in their heart which they intend not to give up, if only because they feel they would not "be" themselves any longer, if they did "not keep some portion" of what they "have been hitherto," with the result that they take up only "a pretence of religion instead of the substance." People may "profess in general terms to wish to be changed," but "when it comes to the point, when particular instances of change are presented to us, we shrink from them, and are content to remain unchanged."[15]

The sermons strongly advocate self-examination in the interests of self-knowledge. For unless we understand ourselves, we cannot understand Christianity, and those who profess to believe but "who neglect the duty of habitual self-examination are using words without meaning."

> For it is in proportion as we search our hearts and understand our own nature, that we understand what is meant by an Infinite Governor and Judge; in proportion as we comprehend the nature

of disobedience and our actual sinfulness, that we feel what is the blessing of the removal of sin, redemption, pardon, sanctification, which otherwise are mere words.

This is "real" belief as opposed to "a mere assent, however sincere."[16] Self-deception is seen as one of the great enemies of the Christian life: "the more guilty we are, the less we know it; for the oftener we sin, the less we are distressed at it."[17] But there are much more subtle forms of self-deception which pervert what is otherwise right and true. For example, we may appreciate that "Knowledge is nothing compared with doing; but the *knowing* that knowledge is nothing, we make to be *something*, we make it count, and thus we cheat ourselves." Again, we may be "proud" of our "so-called humility": "Many a man instead of *learning* humility in practice, confesses himself a poor sinner, and next *prides* himself upon the confession." Or we may make confession of our faults "a *substitute* for real repentance," which enables us "to *put off* repentance." The preacher's avowed aim is to lead his hearers "to some true notion of the depths and deceitfulness of the heart, which we do not really know."[18]

A preoccupation with the "real" and the "unreal" runs through the sermons. Most Christians do not "realize" what it is they profess to believe, but content themselves with "an unreal faith," substituting "a mere outward and nominal profession" for "real" belief. An "indolent use of words without apprehending them" is the natural concomitant of a merely "passive faith." Newman insists that all religion "must be *real.*" To profess a religious belief as true, and yet not be able to "feel, think, speak, act as if it were true," is to believe "in an unreal way." The reason people do not "act upon the truths they utter" is that "they do not *realize* what they are so ready to proclaim"; it is only when people "realize a truth" that "it becomes an influential principle within them." Conversely, holy people have "such a remarkable simplicity" and can "speak about themselves . . . in so unaffected a tone" precisely because "they do not feel" their goodness "in that vivid way which we call realizing"—"They do not open their hearts to the knowledge, so that it becomes fruitful." This is why, if the holy person speaks of an injury done to him, "it will be in the same sort of strange, unreal, and (as I may say) forced and unnatural way in which pretenders to religion speak of religious joy and spiritual comfort, for he is as little at home with anger and revenge as hypocrites are with thoughts of heaven."[19]

In one of the most penetrating sermons he ever preached, "Unreal Words," Newman pointed out that when we subscribe to religious beliefs, we have to use words, and "Words have a meaning, whether we mean that meaning or not," so that "To make professions is to play with edged tools, unless we attend to what we are saying." The expression of religious feelings, too, may be unreal, since someone may "*not* really believe" the doctrines of Christianity "absolutely, because such absolute belief is the work of long time, and therefore his profession of feeling outruns the real inward existence of feeling, or he becomes unreal." Unreality also affects religious, like other, knowledge: people who "do not understand the difference between one point and another," who "have no means of judging, no standard to measure by," are in consequence "inconsistent" and "unreal." The conclusion is that "unreality ... is a sin; it is the sin of every one of us, in proportion as our hearts are cold, or our tongues excessive."[20] For God "meant us to be simple, and we are unreal," with the result that "the whole structure of society is ... artificial."[21]

A real religion reveals itself above all in actions as opposed to feelings and words. In "Unreal Words" he remarked that "Literature is almost in its essence unreal; for it is the exhibition of thought disjoined from practice."[22] The point is developed in one of the most interesting of the sermons, "The Danger of Accomplishments," which argues that the danger of a literary education is that "it separates feeling and acting." Newman complains that the effect of reading novels, for example, is that "*We* have nothing *to do;* we read, are affected, softened or roused, and that is all; we cool again,—nothing comes of it." But

> God has made us feel in order that we may *go on to act* in consequence of feeling; if then we allow our feelings to be excited without acting upon them, we do mischief to the moral system within us, just as we might spoil a watch, or other piece of mechanism, by playing with the wheels of it. We weaken its springs, and they cease to act truly.[23]

"It is easy," he remarks in another sermon, for religious people "to make professions, easy to say fine things in speech or in writing, easy to astonish men with truths which they do not know, and sentiments which rise above human nature." But in order to prove that faith is real, "Let not your words run on; force every one of them into action as it goes. . . . "[24] It is not "by giving utterance to religious sentiments" that we "become religious," but "rather the reverse," by "obeying God in practice."[25] To do "one deed of obedience for Christ's sake" is better than any amount of religious eloquence, feeling, and imagination.[26] People who talk of love in general terms come in for some of Newman's sharpest sarcasm:

> Such men have certain benevolent *feelings* towards the world,—feelings and nothing more;—nothing more than unstable feelings, the mere offspring of an indulged imagination, which exist only when their minds are wrought upon, and are sure to fail them in the hour of need. This is not to love men, it is but to talk about love.—The real love of man *must* depend on practice, and therefore, must begin by exercising itself on our friends around us, otherwise it will have no existence.[27]

He condemns "mere feeling" as "a sort of luxury of the imagination," which has no place in this world, which is intended to be "a world of practice and labour," a place for "obedience," not "excellent words."[28]

The realism of the sermons can be quite disconcerting, even shocking. It is true that, as always with Newman, one must guard against selective quotation emphasizing only one side of a question, but there is no doubt that he is remarkably unencouraging and unsanguine about the progress of Christianity in the world. The revival of religion in the nineteenth century did not impress him very much. He owned to being "suspicious of any religion that is a people's religion, or an age's religion." The "token" of "true religion" was rather "The light shining in darkness," and, "though doubtless there are seasons when a sudden enthusiasm arises in favour of the Truth . . . yet such a popularity of the Truth is *but* sudden, comes at once and goes at once, has no regular growth, no abiding stay." It is unfortunately, "error alone which grows and is received heartily on a large scale." Even though truth "has that power in it, that it forces men to profess it in words," still, "when they go on to act, instead of obeying *it*, they substitute some idol in the place of it." In the face of any manifestation of religion, "a cautious mind will feel anxious lest some counterfeit be, in fact, honoured instead of it."[29] The fact of the matter is that people's "real quarrel with religion . . . is not that it is strict, or engrossing, or imperative, not that it goes too far, but that it *is* religion." As for the Church, "she attempts much, she expects and promises little."[30] The idea of a faithful remnant runs through the Bible, and "when Christ came, the bulk of His own people rejected Him."[31] Since then, redemption "*has* come to all the world, but the world is not changed thereby as a whole," for people have to be "changed *one by one*."[32] Christians should have "no vain imaginings about the world's real conversion." Indeed, Jesus spoke of the "Gospel being preached, not chiefly as a means of converting, but as a witness against the world."[33] A realist would have to ask whether the world is not "as unbelieving now as when Christ came," and whether Christians, "except a small remnant," would not, like the Jews, reject Christ if he came again.[34] In spite of all the good influences of Christianity, it has to be admitted that "the great multitude of men have to all appearance remained, in a spiritual point of view, no better than before": the sad fact is that "Human nature remains what it was, though it has been baptized." The "real triumph of the Gospel" has been to raise up a comparatively few "specimens of faith and holiness, which without it are unknown and impossible"—"It has laboured for the elect, and it has succeeded with them."[35] Most Christians, on the other hand, "would go on almost as they do, neither much better nor much worse, if they believed Christianity to be a fable," for, although they "wish to be religious" and "feel a sort of respect for religious men," they "do not get so far as to have any sort of love for religion."[36] For the ordinary person, "true religion" has a monotonous "sameness" and "plainness," for "it is a weariness to the natural man to serve God humbly and in obscurity."[37]

It was perhaps ironic that the sermons should insist with such a deeply pessimistic realism on the Gospel's inherent lack of appeal for fallen man, when the very same sermons were intended above all else to be "*real*" and to have "reality in them," precisely by bringing out the Gospel in all its concrete actuality.[38] For the preacher's aim was to present the person of Christ not in an "unreal way—as a mere idea or vision," but as "Scripture has set Him before us in His actual sojourn on earth, in His gestures, words, and deeds." Instead of using "vague statements about His love, His willingness to receive the sinner, His imparting repentance and spiritual aid, and the like," the sermons attempt to present "Christ as manifested in the Gospels, the Christ who exists therein, external to our own imaginings . . . really a living being."[39] This was in marked contrast to Evangelical preachers, whom Newman accused of directing "a certain disproportionate attention to the doctrines connected with the work of Christ, in comparison of those which relate to His Person."[40] The Christ of Newman's homilies was not the abstract Christ of the atonement, but the real-life person in the Gospels—someone who "would now be called with contempt a vagrant."[41]

The most famous example of this imaginative realization is to be found in the sermon called "The Incarnate Son, a Sufferer and Sacrifice," where Newman challenges his hearers to read the story of the Passion "without fear and trembling." When Christ was brought before the high priest and struck, "that officer lifted up his hand against God the Son."

> Yes, we shall all of us, for weal or for woe, one day see that holy Countenance which wicked men struck and dishonoured; we shall see those Hands that were nailed to the cross; that Side which was pierced. We shall see all this; and it will be the sight of the Living God.[42]

Years later, one of the congregation, James Anthony Froude, recalled this sermon—although not the exact words—where Newman "described closely some of the incidents of our Lord's passion," and "then paused."

> For a few moments there was a breathless silence. Then, in a low, clear voice, of which the faintest vibration was audible in the farthest corner of St. Mary's, he said, "Now, I bid you recollect that He to whom these things were done was Almighty God." It was as if an electric stroke had gone through the church, as if every person present understood for the first time the meaning of what he had all his life been saying. I suppose it was an epoch in the mental history of more than one of my Oxford contemporaries.[43]

Newman's preaching has often been criticized for its excessive severity, which has been attributed to the Calvinistic Evangelicalism which accompanied and followed his adolescent conversion of 1816. But not only was Newman well aware that his sermons tended in this direction, but the bias was quite deliberate on his part and, far from emanating unconsciously from early influences which he had consciously disowned, the sternness was a studied reaction against Evangelical religion. This is shown very clearly by his treatment of the role of the Holy Spirit in the life of the Christian.

On the one hand, Newman's own reading of the New Testament and the Fathers had led him to discover the great doctrine of the "indwelling" of the Holy Spirit. And this rediscovery, so important for his theology of justification, is certainly to be found in the sermons: "He pervades us . . . as a light pervades a building, or as a sweet perfume the folds of some honourable robe; so that, in Scripture language, we are said to be in Him, and He in us."[44] The mystical note was, Newman claimed, very unlike both the "enthusiasm" of Evangelicals and the "coldness" and "dryness" of liberal and high-and-dry Anglicans: "Till we understand that the gifts of grace are unseen, supernatural, and mysterious, we have but a choice between explaining away the high and glowing expressions of Scripture, or giving them that rash, irreverent, and self-exalting interpretation, which is one of the chief errors of this time." The alternative to the assumption that "the gift of the Holy Ghost was almost peculiar to the Apostles' day, that now, at least, it does nothing more than make us decent and orderly members of society," did not have to be "a sort of religious ecstasy . . . a high-wrought sensibility on sacred subjects . . . impassioned thoughts, a soft and languid tone of feeling, and an unnatural profession of all this in conversation."[45] In spite of the mystery of the invisible "indwelling" of the third Person of the Trinity, and therefore necessarily of the other two Persons also, Newman is emphatic that there is nothing in the least bit unreal about this supernatural relationship—"we are assured of some real though mystical fellowship with the Father, Son, and Holy Spirit . . . so that . . . by a real presence in the soul . . . God is one with every believer, as in a consecrated Temple."[46]

On the other hand, in spite of his high theology of the Holy Spirit, Newman in his sermons deliberately plays down the importance of the Spirit in the Christian life. This lack of emphasis was noted critically when the first volume of Parochial Sermons was published in 1834. In answer to criticism from Evangelicals, Newman explained that he preached as he did because he believed the Spirit normally worked through ordinary human channels, such as the conscience, reason, and feelings, but "does not come immediately to change us." It was in this sense that Newman could even say that "salvation depends on ourselves"—an expression that was

bound to be startling, to say the least, to those who believed
in justification by faith alone. Consequently, in his preaching
he had been "led" to "enlarge on our part of the work not on
the Spirit's," since he was convinced that what needed to be
emphasized was "*the Law* not the Gospel in this age—we want
rousing—we want the claims of duty and the details of obedience set before us strongly." It was, of course, true that Christian works had to be done "through the Spirit," but that did
not alter the fact that they had to be done by ordinary human
means. This was something "this age forgets," which was why
it was "necessary to bring out the fact in all its details before
the world." Evangelicalism had led people to assume "that a
saving state is one, where the mind merely looks to Christ,"
with the result that actual moral behavior could seem to be
virtually irrelevant.[47] The act of accepting that Jesus was one's
personal savior, together with the accompanying feelings
which testified to the sincerity of one's faith, had come to be
seen as the hallmarks of the real Christian. Newman was
intent on showing that such a conversion might be the beginning but was certainly not the end of the Christian life. The
severity of his preaching, therefore, has everything to do with
his own conscious and deliberate rejection of Evangelicalism,
and very little, if anything, to do with any latent Calvinistic
puritanism that might have survived his deconversion. Sermons that were mostly concerned with preaching the atonement and faith in the saving Christ seemed to Newman to
encourage an antinomianism that threatened the growth of
any real spirituality.

In his actual preaching Newman was quite unrepentant:
"Doubtless many a one there is, who, on hearing doctrines
such as I have been insisting on, says in his heart, that religion
is thus made gloomy and repulsive; that he would attend to a
preacher who spoke in a less severe way; and that in fact
Christianity was not intended to be a dark burdensome law,
but a religion of cheerfulness and joy." It was not just that he
wanted to stress the stern side of Christianity in opposition
to the religious spirit of the age, but, as in all his thinking,

he was anxious to pursue an integrative approach and to avoid stressing any one aspect at the expense of the whole. In order to highlight the bright side of Christianity, it was essential, Newman thought, to see the dark side: "we must fear and be in sorrow, before we can rejoice. The Gospel must be a burden before it comforts and brings us peace."[48]

If there was more emphasis on the one side than the other in his preaching, this was because this aspect had been obscured and needed stressing, not only to do justice to it but also to set the other aspect in relief: if the light was to shine, it must cast its own shadow. Without severity, Christian love is likely to degenerate into a counterfeit of itself: "I wish I saw any prospect of this element of zeal and holy sternness springing up among us, to temper and give character to the languid, unmeaning benevolence which we misname Christian love." Christian morality, Newman insists, forms one whole and involves "the reconciling in our conduct opposite virtues," as opposed to cultivating "single virtues."[49]

The integration of love and severity only reflects the whole redemptive action of Christ, who both died and rose for sinners, so that Christians must observe both Good Friday and Easter, both sorrow at the Crucifixion and rejoice at the Resurrection—a "union of opposite thoughts" which "is impressed on us in Holy Communion, in which we see Christ's death and resurrection together, at one and the same time."[50] Again, without the sorrow the joy will be muted: "None rejoice in Easter-tide less than those who have not grieved in Lent." The paradox is that "previous humiliation sobers our joy," while "it alone secures it to us."[51] Similarly, "The duty of fearing does but perfect our joy; that joy alone is true Christian joy, which is informed and quickened by fear, and made thereby sober and reverent."[52] But, it is important to stress, the opposite is equally true for Newman: "Gloom is no Christian temper; that repentance is not real, which has not love in it; that self-chastisement is not acceptable, which is not sweetened by . . . cheerfulness. We must live in sunshine, even when we sorrow . . . "[53] Belief in the Ascension involves a similar emotional conflict as belief in the Crucifixion and Ressurection, for "Christ's going to the Father is at once a source of sorrow, because it involves His absence; and of joy, because it involves His presence."

And so out of the doctrines of the redemption "spring those Christian paradoxes, often spoken of in Scripture, that we are sorrowing, yet always rejoicing; as having nothing, yet possessing all things."[54] For "it is a paradox how the Christian should in all things be sorrowful yet always rejoicing, and dying yet living, and having nothing yet possessing all things."[55] Holiness itself involves the sharpest apparent contradictions for the simple reason that holiness implies the wholeness of the Christian life, so that "the most holy" are those who "confess themselves the most sinful; who ever seek to please Him, yet feel they never can; who are full of good works, yet of works of penance."[56] This tension of opposites is as characteristic of Newman's thought as is their integration as parts of a larger whole.

Another factor, finally, which accounts for the severity of the sermons is, of course, as we have already seen, their relentless realism, particularly their psychological penetration. "He seemed," Froude recalled, "to be addressing the most secret consciousness of each of us—as the eyes of a portrait appear to look at every person in a room."[57] An obvious aspect of the unreal nature of so many people's professed Christianity is inconsistency. (When we come to look at Newman's satirical art, we shall see how the inconsistent is practically synonymous with the unreal). Such lack of consistency is a "scandal" because there is no greater "antecedent prejudice against religion" than the inconsistent "lives of its professors."[58] But no one understood better than Newman the fluctuations of the heart that permitted such inconsistency:

> How difficult it is to remain firm and in one mind under the seductions or terrors of the world! We feel variously according to the place, time, and people we are with. We are serious on Sunday, and we sin deliberately on Monday. We rise in the

morning with remorse at our offences and resolutions of amend-
ment, yet before night we have transgressed again. The mere
change of society puts us into a new frame of mind. . . .[59]

There is no guaranteeing human consistency: "We can never
answer how we shall act under new circumstances."[60] As so
often, Newman turns to Scripture to illustrate his psychological insight into the insidious nature of inconsistency, lurking
in the very midst of consistency:

> if we look to some of the most eminent saints of Scripture, we
> shall find their recorded errors to have occurred in those parts
> of their duty in which each had had most trial, and generally
> showed obedience most perfect. *Faithful* Abraham through want
> of faith denied his wife. Moses, the *meekest* of men, was excluded
> from the land of promise for a passionate word. The *wisdom* of
> Solomon was seduced to bow down to idols. Barnabas again, the
> *son of consolation,* had a sharp contention with St. Paul.[61]

It is because, Newman warns grimly, there are "such inconsistencies in the heart and life of even the better sort of men,
that continual repentance must ever go hand in hand with
our endeavours to obey."[62] The preoccupation with inconsistency is a constant, even obsessive, feature of the sermons:
"Even the most matured saints . . . could they have been
thoroughly scanned even by man, would . . . have exhibited
inconsistencies such as to surprise and shock their most ardent
disciples."[63] Given "the inconsistencies of even the holiest
and most perfect," it is not surprising that "consistent obedience is a very rare endowment," which certainly does not
belong to the ordinary run of people: "How common it is for
men to have *seasons* of seriousness, how exact is their devotion
during them, how suddenly they come to an end, how completely all traces of them vanish, yet how comparatively tri-
fling is the cause of the relapse, a change of place or occupa-
tion, or a day's interruption of regularity in their religious
course!"[64]

Newman has his own penetrating explanation for much of

our apparently involuntary inconsistency: to past "single or forgotten sins . . . are not improbably to be traced the strange inconsistencies of character which we often witness in our experience of life. I mean, you meet continually with men possessed of a number of good points, amiable and excellent men, yet in one respect perhaps strangely perverted."[65] Nor is it enough to have repented once, as psychological insight rather than severity compels Newman to point out: "Thus do past years rise up against us in present offences; gross inconsistencies show themselves in our character; and much need have we continually to implore God to forgive us our past transgressions, which still live in spite of our repentance, and act of themselves vigorously against our better mind, feebly influenced by that younger principle of faith, by which we fight against them."[66]

Newman may have abandoned Evangelicalism, but he had learned much from the kind of rigorous self-analysis which the Evangelical habit of self-examination inculcated and which was strongly encouraged by such standard spiritual guides as William Wilberforce's *Practical View* (1797) and Hannah More's *Practical Piety* (1811). To the extent that this type of spiritual introspection replaced a Christocentric spirituality, Newman rejected it, but it was surely as important for the psychological discernment of his own sermons as it was significant for the creative achievement of another ex-Evangelical, the novelist George Eliot, whose subtle probing of intention and motive, and especially of self-delusion, was to raise the delineation of character in the novel to an altogether new level. Again, then, it is not puritanical gloom or Calvinistic pessimism which has affected Newman's preaching, but rather an element which he has borrowed from his Evangelical background and adapted for his own somewhat different purpose. Just as he came to reject the absolute division Evangelicals were wont to make between so-called "nominal" and "real" Christians, but without abandoning the concept of the "real" to characterize his own very different idea of Christian spirituality; so too an emphasis on introspection is retained, not to

foster "self-contemplation" but to encourage an abandonment
of self through true Christian asceticism.

Certainly, Newman's power of psychological analysis is intended to have a devastating effect on the kind of spiritual
complacency that was the chief target of his preaching. Outward behavior, however good, for example, is no guarantee
of anything:

> it is quite evident that so very much of our apparent obedience
> to God arises from mere obedience to the world and its fashions.
> . . . Let a person merely reflect on the number and variety of bad
> or foolish thoughts which he suffers, and dwells on in private,
> which he would be ashamed to put into words, and he will at
> once see, how very poor a test his outward demeanour in life is
> of his real holiness in the sight of God. [67]

As for ordinary moral respectability, Newman has no doubt
that no credit is due to religious faith: "It is plain, as a matter
of fact, that the great mass of men are protected from gross sin
by the forms of society. The received laws of propriety and
decency, the prospect of a loss of character, stand as sentinels,
giving the alarm, long before their *Christian* principles have
time to act." [68] Our motives are always suspect: "Do we not
support religion for the sake of peace and good order?" [69] The
world may praise consistency, but its idea of consistency is
hardly very consistent: "a man is conscientious and consistent,
who is only inconsistent and goes against conscience in any
extremity, when hardly beset, and when he must cut the knot
or remain in present difficulties. That is, *he* is thought to obey
conscience, who only disobeys it when it is a praise and merit
to obey it." The reluctant determination of the world to be
inconsistent is analyzed with biting irony:

> This, alas! is the way with some of the most honourable of mere
> men of the world, nay of the mass of (so called) respectable
> men. They never tell untruths, or break their word, or profane
> the Lord's day, or are dishonest in trade, or falsify their princi-
> ples, or insult religion, except in very great straits or great emer-

gencies, when driven into a corner; and then perhaps they force
themselves . . . and (as it were) undergo their sin as a sort of
unpleasant self-denial or penance, being ashamed of it all the
while, getting it over as quickly as they can, shutting their eyes
and leaping blindfold, and then forgetting it, as something which
is bitter to think about. [70]

One psychological lesson the sermons never tire of repeat-
ing concerns the part habit plays in our moral and spiritual
lives. Newman's great common-sense maxim is that the more
we try to be good, the better we become: "We must become
what we are not; we must learn to love what we do not love,
and practise ourselves in what is difficult." [71] But the difficulty
lies precisely in forming new good habits when old bad habits
are still dominant. For God's forgiveness does not remove the
effects of sin: "God may forgive, but the sin has had its work,
and its memento is set up in the soul." [72] And Newman is
especially unsentimental about "the sins of our youth," by
which "the power of the flesh is exerted against us, as a second
creative principle of evil, aiding the malice of the Devil." [73]
As a result, those who have serious youthful transgressions
on their conscience "must not be surprised if obedience is with
them a laborious up-hill work all their days." [74] Possession of
free will does not remove "the load of corrupt nature and sinful
habits which hang upon [the] will, and clog it in each particular exercise of it." This is why it is mere "self-deception" to
assume that it is possible to delay repentance:

I do not speak of the dreadful presumption of such a mode of
quieting conscience (though many people really use it who do
not speak the words out, or are aware that they act upon it),
but, merely, of the ignorance it evinces concerning our moral
condition, and our power of willing and doing. . . .

So very difficult is obedience, so hardly won is every step in
our Christian course, so sluggish and inert our corrupt nature,
that I would have a man disbelieve he can do one jot or tittle
beyond what he has already done; refrain from borrowing aught
on the hope of the future, however good a security for it he seems

to be able to show; and never take his good feelings and wishes in pledge for one single untried deed. Nothing but *past* acts are the vouchers for future.[75]

On the other hand, the power of habit ("a permanent power in the mind")[76] is such that "obedience to God's commandments is ever easy, and almost without effort to those who begin to serve Him from the beginning of their days; whereas those who wait a while, find it grievous in proportion to their delay."[77] And without any exaggeration, Newman can say, "indefinitely great results may follow from one act of obedience."[78] Even so, "no habit is formed at once."[79]

Part of the power of sin over our lives, however, lies in our own self-deception and self-delusion. "Evil thoughts," for example, "do us no harm, if recognized; if repelled, if protested against by the indignation and self-reproach of the mind. It is when we do not discern them, when we admit them, when we cherish them, that they ripen into principles."[80] But then to some extent self-knowledge is impossible because it is not possible to foresee the developments of sin: "When a man begins to do wrong, he cannot answer for himself how far he may be carried on. He does not see beforehand, he cannot know where he shall find himself after the sin is committed. One false step forces him to another, for retreat is impossible."[81] And Newman leaves us in no doubt that there is an ignorance of the implications of sin which is bliss: "Did we see the complete consequences of any one sin, did we see how it spreads by the contagion of example and influence through the world, how many souls it injures, and what its eternal effects are, doubtless we should become speechless and motionless, as though we saw the flames of hell fire."[82]

Much less desirable and much more dangerous is that quasi-deliberate amnesia about the sins of our past lives which makes people speak with "sometimes even something of tenderness and affection for their former selves;—or at best they speak of themselves in a sort of moralizing way, as they might of sinners they read of, as if it were not now *their* concern what

they then were. . . . "[83] But some self-ignorance is quite unconscious, as in someone "who goes on, for years perhaps, and
no one ever discovers his particular failings, nor does he know
them himself; till at length he is brought into certain circumstances, which bring them out." Sometimes we are not aware
of the hidden relation between particular sins, so that "single
sins indulged or neglected are often the cause of other defects
of character, which seem to have no connexion with them,
but which after all are rather symptomatic of the former, than
themselves at the bottom of the mischief." Again, a person
usually has "some besetting sin or other . . . and this one
indulged infirmity may in consequence be producing most
distressing effects on his spiritual state . . . without his being
aware of it," until he "gradually" learns "to palliate, or rather
account for, on other principles, to refer to other motives, to
justify on religious or other grounds."[84]

One common form of self-deception is to try and persuade
oneself that one has not sinned—"Sinful feelings and passions
generally take upon themselves the semblance of reason, and
affect to argue." Accordingly, it is not surprising that "Our
first parents were as ready with excuses, as their posterity
when Christ came."[85] The preacher does not hesitate to con-
front his hearers with the harsh truth that real repentance
may even be psychologically impossible: "You cannot bear to
be other than you are. Life would seem a blank to you, were
you other. . . . "[86] For "easy as it is to avoid sin first of all, at
length it is (humanly speaking) impossible."[87] Once again,
many of our involuntary sins arise out of our past sins:

> We cannot rid ourselves of sin when we would; though we re-
> pent, though God forgives us, yet it remains in its power over
> our souls, in our habits, and in our memories. It has given a
> colour to our thoughts, words, and works; and though, with
> many efforts, we would wash it out from us, yet this is not
> possible except gradually.

Newman does not hesitate to use terrifying images to convey
the compulsive nature of such sinning in people who have

genuinely repented of previous habits of sin "and would fain be other than they have been, but their former self clings to them, as a poisoned garment, and eats into them." The pain is exacerbated by "those sins which rise from the devil's temptations, inflaming the wounds and scars of past sins healed, or nearly so; exciting the memory, and hurrying us away; and thus making use of our former selves against our present selves contrary to our will."[88]

Such probings into the most sensitive parts of the psyche cannot help but remind readers of George Eliot's novels of her own dramatic explorations of moral weakness, which culminate in the tragic portrait of the Evangelical banker, Mr Bulstrode, in her greatest novel, *Middlemarch*. If Newman's sermons fail to reach the same level of literary artistry, we may at least partly blame the form in which he was writing; but there is no question that the English sermon had never before and has never since attained such psychological intensity and subtlety.

4

THE THEOLOGIAN

As A CATHOLIC, NEWMAN ALWAYS disavowed any claim to be a theologian. His comparative ignorance of the theology of the schools made him feel that he had no right to claim to be a professional theologian. In fact, his own first essay in ecclesiology, which was to be the major theological contribution of his Catholic period, happened almost by chance. His Anglican theological writings were founded on his profound study of Scripture and the Fathers, especially the Greek Fathers, which far exceeded such knowledge as he had come to have of St. Thomas and the Schoolmen and of post-Tridentine theology. Since the teaching of the Second Vatican Council, which arose out of and which in turn stimulated a return to the sources of the Church's theology, Newman's deeply scriptural and patristic thought has come into its own among Catholic theologians. The ecumenical attractions of the most seminal of modern Catholic theologians, whose thinking is so markedly un-Scholastic, are also clear enough.

I

We have already seen how Newman's essential philosophical ideas, which received their final expression in the *Grammar of Assent,* came early to him. In the same way we find his most characteristic theological themes already exhibited in his

first book, *The Arians of the Fourth Century* (1833). For Newman the Arians were like the religious liberals of his own day
both in their misapplication of human reason to the mysteries
of revelation and in their objection to using nonscriptural
terminology in credal statements. The doctrinal "comprehensiveness" that broad Anglicans like Thomas Arnold were
advocating is brusquely rejected: "If the Church would be
vigorous and influential, it must be decided and plain-spoken
in its doctrine. . . . To attempt comprehensions of opinion . . .
is to mistake arrangements of words, which have no existence
except on paper, for . . . realities; and ingenious generalizations of discordant sentiments for that practical agreement
which alone can lead to co-operation." While it is only realistic to acknowledge that "there are no two opinions so contrary
to each other, but some form of words may be found vague
enough to comprehend them both," comprehensiveness is impractical because it is unreal: "We may indeed artificially clas-
sify light and darkness under one term or formula; but nature
has her own fixed courses. . . . However plausible may be the
veil thus thrown over heterogeneous doctrines, the flimsy arti-
fice is discomposed so soon as the principles beneath it are
called upon to move and act." In fact, comprehensiveness,
Newman claims, is harmful to the Church because of its unreal substitution of "words for things" in the form of "statements so faintly precise and so decently ambiguous, as to
embrace the greatest number of opinions possible, and to de-
prive religion, in consequence, of its austere and commanding
aspect."[1]

As in other areas of Newman's thought, the touchstone is
whether something is real or unreal: so much so that to ask
whether a thing is true or not, is in effect to ask whether it is
real or unreal. Alongside the insistence on the need for a
"view," there runs through Newman's writings a deep distrust
of the merely notional or theoretical. And, as in his philosophy, there is a sharp distinction made between "things" and
"words," with the strong implication that the former is greatly
preferable. The test of an idea or proposition is a pragmatic

test: what is the reality to which it corresponds and what, if any, are its practical consequences?

In addition to this congenital suspicion of mere words, Newman had a theological sense of the inadequacy of human language that came from his study of the Alexandrian Church's "mystical or sacramental principle," which, he was to explain in the *Apologia*, meant that the Church's dogmas "are but the expressions in human language of truths to which the human mind is unequal."[2] Doctrine, as he put it in *The Arians*, should be seen as only "the shadow, projected for the contemplation of the intellect, of the Object of scripturally-informed piety: a representation, economical; necessarily imperfect, as being exhibited in a foreign medium, and therefore involving apparent inconsistencies or mysteries." A "systematic" dogma could be "kept in the background in the infancy of Christianity, when faith and obedience were vigorous," and only "brought forward at a time when, reason being disproportionately developed, and aiming at sovereignty in the province of religion, its presence became necessary to expel an usurping idol from the house of God." From the individual believer's point of view, to make explicit what was implicit was not necessarily desirable: "so reluctant is a well-constituted mind to reflect on its own motive principles, that the correct intellectual image, from its hardness of outline, may startle and offend those who have all along been acting upon it." Far from dogmatic formularies being attractive for their own sake, Newman insists that "freedom from symbols and articles is abstractedly the highest state of Christian communion, and the peculiar privilege of the primitive Church," for "technicality and formalism are, in their degree, inevitable results of public confessions of faith," and "when confessions do not exist, the mysteries of divine truth, instead of being exposed to the gaze of the profane and uninstructed, are kept hidden in the bosom of the Church, far more faithfully than is otherwise possible." Accordingly, "the rulers of the Church were dilatory in applying a remedy, which nevertheless the circumstances of the times imperatively required. They were

loath to confess, that the Church had grown too old to enjoy
the free, unsuspicious teaching with which her childhood was
blest. . . ."

And so dogmatic formulations became necessary, and Newman does not in any way attempt to minimize their importance. Indeed, the fact that "we cannot restrain the rovings
of the intellect, or silence its clamorous demand for a formal
statement concerning the Object of our worship" means paradoxically that the insistence that "intellectual representation
should ever be subordinate to the cultivation of the religious
affections" actually involves the "intellectual expression of
theological truth," not only because it "excludes heresy," but
because it "directly assists the acts of religious worship and
obedience."[3]

The alternative, then, to comprehensiveness is not dogmatism. Instead, a characteristically careful balance between opposing extremes is maintained. On the one hand, the inherent inadequacy of religious language is readily recognized, as
well as the drawback of attempting to describe the ineffable.
On the other hand, not only is the necessity of some kind of
verbal formulation acknowledged, but its virtue for religious
practice is also admitted.

Among the "various Economics or Dispensations of the
Eternal" involved in the "sacramental principle" was the "dispensation . . . in favour of the Gentiles," whereby "pagan
literature, philosophy, and mythology . . . were but a preparation for the Gospel."[4] The possibility of revelation outside
Christianity was not familiar to Newman's contemporaries,
nor was the idea current among Roman Catholics before the
Second Vatican Council. But again it is highly characteristic
of Newman that in the midst of his inflexible opposition to
doctrinal liberalism and heresy, he could introduce suddenly
an element of surprise by declaring unequivocally: "There
never was a time when God had not spoken to man, and told
him to a certain extent his duty." It was true that "the Church
of God ever has had, and the rest of mankind never have
had, authoritative documents of truth, and appointed chan-

nels of communication with Him . . . but all men have had
more or less the guidance of Tradition, in addition to those
internal notions of right and wrong which the Spirit has put
into the heart of each individual." Newman calls this "vague
and uncertain family of religious truths, originally from God,
but sojourning without the sanction of miracle, or a definite
home, as pilgrims up and down the world, and discernible and
separable from the corrupt legends with which they are mixed
. . . the *Dispensation of Paganism.*" There is therefore "nothing
unreasonable in the notion, that there may have been heathen poets and sages, or sibyls again, in a certain sense di-
vinely illuminated, and organs through whom religious and
moral truth was conveyed." This is why the Christian missionary should "after St. Paul's manner, seek some points in the
existing superstitions as the basis of his own instructions, instead of indiscriminately condemning and discarding the
whole assemblage of heathen opinions and practices," thus
"recovering and purifying, rather than reversing the essential
principles of their belief."[5]

The tension between different points of view or aspects of
a question which is so marked a feature of Newman's thought
can be seen two years later in his *Tract 73* (1835), afterwards
to be republished as "On the Introduction of Rationalistic
Principles into Revealed Religion." Rationalism is first defined as an "abuse" of reason, "that is, a use of it for purposes
for which it never was intended, and is unfitted."

> To rationalize in matters of Revelation is to make our reason the
> standard and measure of the doctrines revealed; to stipulate that
> those doctrines should be such as to carry with them their own
> justification; to reject them, if they come in collision with our
> existing opinions or habits of thought, or are with difficulty
> harmonized with our existing stock of knowledge.

And yet there is, Newman freely acknowledges, a legitimate
use of reason in religious inquiry, as the sharply antithetical
rhetoric of the following energetic passage makes clear:

As regards Revealed Truth, it is not Rationalism to set about to ascertain, by the use of reason, what things are ascertainable by reason, and what are not; nor, in the absence of an express Revelation, to inquire into the truths of Religion, as they come to us by nature; nor to determine what proofs are necessary for the acceptance of a Revelation, if it be given; nor to reject a Revelation on the plea of insufficient proof; nor, after recognizing it as divine, to investigate the meaning of its declarations, and to interpret its language. . . . This is not Rationalism; but it is Rationalism to accept the Revelation, and then to explain it away; to speak of it as the Word of God, and to treat it as the word of man; to refuse to let it speak for itself; to claim to be told the *why* and the *how* of God's dealings with us . . . and to assign to Him a motive and a scope of our own; to stumble at the partial knowledge of what He may give us of them; to put aside what is obscure, as if it had not been said at all; to accept one half of what has been told us, and not the other half; to assume that the contents of Revelation are also its proof; to frame some gratuitous hypothesis about them, and then to garble, gloss, and colour them, to trim, clip, pare away, and twist them, in order to bring them into conformity with the idea to which we have subjected them.

As in *The Arians*, Newman is saved from falling into the opposite kind of rationalism, an overly systematic approach to revelation, by a profound sense of the mystery of Christianity. "Considered as a Mystery," revelation "is a doctrine enunciated by inspiration, in human language, as the only possible medium of it, and suitably, according to the capacity of language; a doctrine *lying hid* in language, to be received in that language from the first by every mind, whatever be its separate power of understanding it . . . . "6 Again, the necessity of verbal formulations is admitted, but the inevitable inadequacy of language is also recognized, as well as the limitations of human thought.

As the Tractarian Movement progressed, it became a matter of pressing urgency to distinguish Anglicanism from Roman Catholicism. And so Newman began to construct the theology of the so-called "Via Media." But he was well aware of the accusation that Anglo-Catholicism might be called a mere *theory*:

> a fine-drawn theory, which has never been owned by any body of churchmen, never witnessed in operation in any system. Laud's attempt was so unsuccessful as to prove he was working upon a mere theory. The actual English Church has never adopted it: in spite of the learning of her divines, she has ranked herself among the Protestants, and the doctrine of the Via Media has slept in libraries.

It could easily be said that, unlike the Roman Catholic and the Protestant,

> when a man takes up this Via Media, he is a mere doctrinarian— he is wasting his efforts in delineating an invisible phantom; and he will be judged, and fairly, to be trifling, and bookish, and unfit for the world. He will be set down in the number of those who, in some matter of business, start up to suggest their own little crotchet, and are for ever measuring mountains with a pocket ruler, or improving the planetary courses. The world moves forward in bold and intelligible parties; it has its roads to the east and north. . . .

In this imaginary dialogue (1836) the narrator's interlocutor advocates reunion with Rome, but the narrator, who stands for the author, judges such "speculations" to be *"unreal."*[7] For Newman there could be no more damning criticism; but what is so remarkable is that it is also precisely the charge which the interlocutor is allowed to make against the "Via Media," which is branded as unreal because it has never been realized in practice.

Whatever misgivings Newman may have had did not stop him from publishing in 1837 his major ecclesiological work on the "Via Media," his *Lectures on the Prophetical Office of the Church viewed relatively to Romanism and Popular Protestantism.*

But at the very outset of the book it is acknowledged that the fact that the "Via Media" is only a "theory" raises a serious objection:

> A religious principle or idea, however true, before it is found in a substantive form, is but a theory; and since many theories are not more than theories, and do not admit of being carried into effect, it is exposed to the suspicion of being one of these, and of having no existence out of books.

However, Newman claims, it does not follow that a theory unrealized in fact is necessarily unreal: "The proof of reality in a doctrine is its holding together when actually attempted." Christianity itself would have seemed "at first a mere literature, or philosophy, or mysticism ... till it was tried." But although the doctrines of the "Via Media" purport to be the "foundation" on which the Christian religion "originally spread," still, since they "related to extremes which did not then exist, and do exist now, they appear unreal, for a double reason, having no exact counterpart in early times, and being superseded now by actually existing systems." The inseparable and damaging truth is that

> Protestantism and Popery are real religions ... but the *Via Media*, viewed as an integral system, has never had existence except on paper; it is known, not positively but negatively, in its differences from the rival creeds, not in its own properties; and can only be described as a third system, neither the one nor the other, but with something of each, cutting between them, and, as if with a critical fastidiousness, trifling with them both, and boasting to be nearer Antiquity than either.

It is noticeable that the author's anxiety is not that the "Via Media" is not *true*, but his uneasy fear that it is not *real* is palpably present in the sarcastic skepticism which he imagines in the minds of detached observers:

> What is this but to fancy a road over mountains and rivers, which has never been cut? When we profess our *Via Media*, as

the very truth of the Apostles, we seem to bystanders to be mere antiquarians or pedants, amusing ourselves with illusions or learned subtleties, and unable to grapple with things as they are.

However many learned theologians may have "propounded" it, "whatever its merits, still, when left to itself . . . it may not 'work.'" Indeed, "the very circumstance that it has been propounded for centuries by great names, and not yet reduced to practice as a system, is alleged as an additional presumption against its feasibility." Frankly admitting the "force" of the objections, Newman insists that "it still remains to be tried whether what is called Anglo-Catholicism . . . is capable of being professed, acted on, and maintained on a larger sphere of action and through a sufficient period, or whether it be a mere modification or transition-state either of Romanism or of popular Protestantism."

The reader is left in no doubt that Anglo-Catholics are "certainly" required "to exhibit" their "principles in action."[8] The thinker who wrote "Life is for action"[9] is not simply concerned that theory should lead to praxis; but rather the validity of the theory depends on the possibility of its implementation in practice. Preeminently pragmatic as a theologian, Newman could not contemplate a theology that was out of touch with reality—and that meant not only facts but also the world of action. This is why he takes comfort from the argument that, while the liberal and puritan parties in the Church of England "have been shown to be but modifications" of Unitarianism and Calvinism "by their respective histories, whenever allowed to act freely," the Anglo-Catholic party, "when it had the opportunity of running into Romanism, in fact did not coalesce with it"—a consideration that suggests "some real differences in it from that system with which it is popularly confounded." However, it may still be objected that the "Via Media," because it has never been properly "brought into operation," is therefore "open to the suspicion of . . . being . . . a mere theory or fancy." Nevertheless, even if Anglo-Catholicism has never been "practically reduced to system

in its fulness, it does exist, in all its parts, in the writings of
our divines, and in good measure is in actual operation." And
so what is vitally needed is an "inventory of our treasures,"
not for the academic purpose of constructing a systematic
theology but for a very practical reason—"We have more than
we know how to use; stores of learning, but little that is
precise and serviceable. . . . "[10] At the end of 1843 Newman
pointed out in a private letter that he had made it clear in the
Prophetical Office that he was afraid "lest the view should prove
a mere paper view, a fine theory, which would not work,
which would not move."[11] But if Newman found himself
forced to abandon the ecclesiology of the "Via Media," the
preoccupation with the real, in the sense of the actual and the
practical, was to be carried forward into his Catholic theology
of the Church.

The most significant part of the *Prophetical Office* is where
Newman makes a key distinction between two kinds of tradition, attempting as he does so to uphold the importance of
tradition without damaging the uniqueness of Scripture. The
Protestant insistence on "the Bible as the only standard of
appeal in doctrinal inquiries" seems to be "an unreal doctrine"
since "the Bible is not so written as to force its meaning upon
the reader," nor does it "carry with it its own interpretation."
Newman wants to mediate between this position and what
he takes to be the Roman Catholic view that tradition provides an extra and independent source of revelation, by doing
justice to both points of view. And, in a very characteristic
way, he does so by introducing a third element which sheds
light on the problem by putting it in a new perspective. He
divides tradition into "Episcopal Tradition," which is derived
from the Apostles, and "Prophetical Tradition," which consists of the interpretation of the revelation, a "body of Truth,
pervading the Church like an atmosphere," and "existing primarily in the bosom of the Church itself, and recorded in such
measure as Providence has determined in the writings of emi-
nent men." It is this latter kind of tradition which may be
"corrupted in its details," so that the doctrines which develop

out of it "are entitled to very different degrees of credit." This perception of "Prophetical Tradition," Newman claims, is in keeping with "the Tradition of the Fathers," which "witnesses" not only "to its own inferiority to Scripture," but also to the fact that "Scripture is the record" and "the sole record of saving truth."[12]

The attempt to find a third or middle way between Protestantism and Tridentine Roman Catholicism also led Newman to write his *Lectures on Justification* (1838), which some would claim is his most acute and profound theological work. He begins by saying that the lectures were intended to show that "certain essential Christian truths, such as Baptismal Regeneration and the Apostolical Ministry," are not in fact "incompatible with the doctrine of justifying grace."[13] In other words, it is another effort to steer a "Via Media" between the "erroneous" idea of justification by "faith only" and the "defective" theory of "justification by obedience." These two "rigid" and "extreme" views, we are told, are both partially right, for the idea that "we are absolutely saved by obedience, that is, by *what we are,* has introduced the proper merit of good works; that we are absolutely saved by faith, or by *what Christ is,* the notion that good works are not conditions of our salvation."[14] But Newman thinks that the Roman "scheme of doctrine" is more nearly right for it "is not unsound or dangerous in itself, but in a certain degree incomplete,—truth, but not the whole truth." This is the view that "justification consists in love, or sanctity, or obedience," and that to be justified is not just to be counted righteous but actually to be made righteous—"not a change merely in God's dealings towards us, like the pale and wan sunshine of a winter's day, but . . . the possession of Himself."[15] We should not be surprised that for Newman there is one decisive consideration: "it is what the rival doctrine is not, a real doctrine, and contains an intelligible, tangible, practical view which one can take and use."[16] By contrast, the Protestant "idea of faith" is dismissed as "a mere theory," with the result that "their whole theology is shadowy and unreal." The theme of reality is developed with striking imagery:

> The one view then differs from the other as the likeness of a man differs from the original. The picture resembles him; but it is not he. It is not a reality, it is all surface. It has no depth, no substance; touch it, and you will find it is not what it pretends to be. . . . I wish to deal with things, not with words. I do not look to be put off with a name or a shadow. I would treat of faith as it is actually found in the soul; and I say it is as little an isolated grace, as a man is a picture. It has a depth, a breadth, and a thickness; it has an inward life which is something over and above itself; it has a heart, and blood, and pulses, and nerves, though not upon the surface. . . . Love and fear and obedience are not really posterior to justifying faith for even a moment of time, unless bones or muscles are formed after the countenance and complexion. It is as unmeaning to speak of living faith, as being independent of newness of mind, as of solidity as divisible from body, or tallness from stature, or colour from the landscape. As well might it be said that an arm or a foot can exist out of the body, and that man is born with only certain portions, head or heart, and that the rest accrues afterwards, as that faith comes first and gives birth to other graces.[17]

There is no need to argue that the Protestant theory of justification by faith is false; it is for Newman enough to have shown that it is unreal and insubstantial.

Are the Protestant and the Roman the only ways of understanding justification? Newman thinks not, for two reasons: first, the classical Anglican divines contrive to combine both approaches in their view of the subject; second, he has his own individual understanding of the matter, which is only original to the extent that it is a rediscovery of what has been forgotten or lost.

Newman argues that the word *justifying* means literally "'counting righteous,' but includes *under* its meaning 'making righteous.'"[18] By "calling righteous what is not righteous till

He calls it so," God not only declares we are justified, but "He *justifies* us."[19] After all, it would be "a strange paradox to say that a thing is not because He says it is."[20] Instead, it is characteristic of God's word in Scripture that it "effects what it announces."[21] Justification, therefore, means both God's *"justifying"* and man's *"being justified,"* just as "work" means "both the doing and the thing done;" and while Protestants usually use the word in the first active sense, and Roman theologians employ it in the second passive sense, in Anglican writers there is no attempt to separate "the seal and the impression, justification and renewal."[22]

But Newman has his own distinct understanding of the problem. For when he comes to consider what essentially justification consists of, he dismisses both the standard Protestant and Roman answers as superficial and unsatisfactory. For if "the inward principle of acceptance" is understood to be faith, then "the question rises, what gives to faith its acceptableness?" And the answer must be that the reason why faith rather than unbelief is "acceptable" is that the former has "a something in it" which the latter does not have, namely, "God's grace." Accordingly, we are bound to conclude that "having that grace or that presence, and not faith, which is its result, must be the real token, the real state of a justified man." On the other hand, "if we say that justification consists in a supernatural quality imparted to the soul by God's grace, as Roman writers say, then in like manner, the question arises" whether "this renovating principle" does not necessarily involve "grace itself, as an immediate divine power or presence." But if this is the case, "then surely the possession of that grace is really our justification, and not renewal, or the principle of renewal." Thus it can be shown, "by tracing farther back the lines of thought on which these apparently discordant views are placed," how they in fact "converge" in "an inward divine presence or grace, of which both faith and spiritual renovation are fruits."

There is, then, a third way of understanding justification which does justice to but at the same time transcends the two rival positions, both deeply imbedded in a late medieval Scholastic theology of grace which had lost touch with scriptural and patristic sources. Its originality lies simply in the rediscovery of the New Testament doctrine of the "indwelling" of the Holy Spirit: "the presence of the Holy Ghost shed abroad in our hearts, the Author both of faith and of renewal, this is really that which makes us righteous, and . . . our righteousness is the possession of that presence." Justification, then, "is wrought by the power of the Spirit, or rather by His presence within us," while "faith and renewal are both present also, but as fruits of it."[23] The "connection" between "justification and renewal" is that they are "both included in that one great gift of God, the indwelling of Christ [through the Holy Spirit] in the Christian soul," which constitutes "our justification and sanctification, as its necessary results"—"And the one cannot be separated from the other except in idea, unless the sun's rays can be separated from the sun, or the power of purifying from fire or water."[24]

In refusing simply to accept the traditional Anglican compromise which aimed to comprehend both the two rival theologies, Newman resolves the problem by setting it in a wholly new perspective. By so doing, he actually changes the nature of the question, which can now be looked at in an altogether different form. This kind of approach, whereby opposing positions are undercut by being circumvented, was to be used later very fruitfully by Newman in tackling very sensitive problems in Roman Catholic ecclesiology. Here it is employed to solve a key point of contention between Protestants and Roman Catholics, and as such suggests its considerable potential value as a method in ecumenical theology, to which Newman's book is an early, outstanding contribution.

We must turn now to what is certainly Newman's most famous and seminal work of theology, his *Essay on the Development of Christian Doctrine* (1845), which he left unfinished on his entry into the Roman Catholic Church. It is worth emphasizing the word "essay" in the title, as it would certainly be unhelpful to approach a book which is anyway incomplete as though it were a systematic treatise propounding a formal theory. It is true that it was written on a "view," which Newman says "has at all times, perhaps, been implicitly adopted by theologians," that is, "the Theory of Development of Doctrine." But he prefers to regard it simply as "an hypothesis to account for a difficulty," the "difficulty" being that Christianity has apparently undergone so many changes and variations over the centuries that the question arises whether there has been any "real continuity of doctrine" since the time of the Apostles.[25] It would hardly be possible for Newman to have a systematic theory of development, since he does not regard the actual doctrinal developments which have taken place as being in any way systematic.

> The development . . . of an idea [like Christianity] is not like an investigation worked out on paper, in which each successive advance is a pure evolution from a foregoing, but it is carried on through and by means of communities of men and their leaders and guides; and it employs their minds as its instruments, and depends upon them, while it uses them.[26]

To understand what Newman means by development one has first to understand what he means by an "idea" and its "aspects."

> The idea which represents an object or supposed object is commensurate with the sum total of its possible aspects, however they may vary in the separate consciousness of individuals; and in proportion to the variety of aspects under which it presents itself to various minds is its force and depth, and the argument for its reality. Ordinarily an idea is not brought home to the intellect as objective except through this variety; like bodily substances, which are not apprehended except under the clothing of their properties and results, and which admit of being walked round, and surveyed on opposite sides, and in different perspectives, and in contrary light, in evidence of their reality. And, as views of a material object may be taken from points so remote or so opposed, that they seem at first sight incompatible,

and especially as their shadows will be disproportionate, or even monstrous, and yet all these anomalies will disappear and all these contrarieties be adjusted, on ascertaining the point of vision or the surface of projection in each case; so also all the aspects of an idea are capable of coalition, and of a resolution into the object to which it belongs; and the *prima facie* dissimilitude of its aspects becomes, when explained, an argument for its substantiveness and integrity, and their multiplicity for its originality and power.

The phrase "different perspectives" is especially worth noting: Newman's theory corresponds to his own practice. If an idea can only be viewed under its multiple different aspects, then it is far too complex and elusive to be pinned down or reduced to any system or formal theory. Far from being in any way static, ideas are dynamic (unless, for example, they are mathematical ideas):

> When an idea, whether real or not, is of a nature to arrest and possess the mind, it may be said to have life, that is, to live in the mind which is its recipient. . . . then it is not merely received passively in this or that form into many minds, but it becomes an active principle within them, leading them to an ever-new contemplation of itself, to an application of it in various directions, and a propagation of it on every side.

A living idea grows gradually into "a body of thought," which "will after all be little more than the proper representative of one idea, being in substance what that idea meant from the first, its complete image as seen in a combination of diversified aspects, with the suggestions and corrections of many minds, and the illustration of many experiences." It is the "process . . . by which the aspects of an idea are brought into consistency and form" which Newman calls "its development, being the germination and maturation of some truth or apparent truth on a large mental field." The word *consistency* is significant, since for Newman to be consistent is to be real: and so an apparent development will only be a real develop-

ment if "the assemblage of aspects, which constitute its ultimate shape, really belongs to the idea from which they start."
Far from being passive,

> A development will have this characteristic, that, its action
> being in the busy scene of human life, it cannot progress at all
> without cutting across, and thereby destroying or modifying and
> incorporating with itself existing modes of thinking and operat-
> ing.

A "great idea," Newman adds, "is elicited and expanded by
trial, and battles into perfection and supremacy." The impossibility of providing any schematic blueprint for doctrinal development is clearly indicated in the following famous passage
where the image of the stream is enlisted to provide a counter-
analogy for the way in which ideas are revealed rather than
obscured by development:

> It is indeed sometimes said that the stream is clearest near the
> spring. Whatever use may fairly be made of this image, it does
> not apply to the history of a philosophy or belief, which on the
> contrary is more equable, and purer, and stronger, when its bed
> has become deep, and broad, and full. It necessarily rises out of
> an existing state of things, and for a time savours of the soil. Its
> vital element needs disengaging from what is foreign and tempo-
> rary. . . . It remains perhaps for a time quiescent; it tries, as it
> were, its limbs, and proves the ground under it, and feels its
> way. From time to time it makes essays which fail, and are in
> consequence abandoned. It seems in suspense which way to go;
> it wavers, and at length strikes out in one definite direction. In
> time it enters upon strange territory; points of controversy alter
> their bearing; parties rise and fall around it; dangers and hopes
> appear in new relations; and old principles reappear under new
> forms. It changes with them in order to remain the same. In a
> higher world it is otherwise, but here below to live is to change,
> and to be perfect is to have changed often.[27]

The fact that halfway through the passage the image seems to
change suggests that there is no question of plotting the pro-

gress of a development as one would a road on a map. No diagram is possible because there is no distinct line to be recorded.

Just as the *Grammar of Assent* has often been grossly misinterpreted and undervalued because it has been misunderstood as purporting to be a metaphysical work, so too the *Essay on the Development of Christian Doctrine* can arouse anticipations that are bound to be disappointed if its essentially unsystematic character is not appreciated. Most obviously, the seven "Notes" which Newman proposes to distinguish developments from corruptions have been criticized as unconvincing and uncomprehensive. But Newman sounds more diffident than dogmatic when he introduces them ("I venture to set down ..."),[28] and it is noteworthy how in the second revised edition he substitutes the vaguer, less definite word (*Notes*) for the more rigorous *Tests* of the original first edition. They are not intended to be necessarily in themselves definitive and comprehensive criteria.

In the *Essay* Newman is not attempting to "prove" anything, in the strict sense of that word. Rather, he is concerned with two pictures he has before his mind's eye, that of the modern Roman Catholic Church and that of the early Church. Are these two apparently very dissimilar pictures in fact portraits of one and the same Church? The appeal to the reader is fundamentally to see or recognize a likeness which the author has seen. In other words, to regard the book as a theoretical work is to miss the role which the imagination plays and which, given the nature of Newman's philosophy of the mind, we should expect it to play.

> On the whole, all parties will agree that, of all existing systems, the present communion of Rome is the nearest approximation in fact to the Church of the Fathers, possible though some may think it, to be nearer still to that Church on paper. Did St. Athanasius or St. Ambrose come suddenly to life, it cannot be doubted what communion he would take to be his own. All surely will agree that these Fathers, with whatever opinions of

their own, whatever protests, if we will, would find themselves
more at home with such men as St. Bernard or St. Ignatius
Loyola, or with the lonely priest in his lodging, or the holy
sisterhood of mercy, or the unlettered crowd before the altar,
than with the teachers or with the members of any other creed.
And may we not add, that were those same Saints, who once
sojourned, one in exile, one on embassy, at Treves, to come
more northward still, and to travel until they reached another
fair city, seated among groves, green meadows, and calm
streams, the holy brother would turn from many a high aisle and
solemn cloister which they found there, and ask the way to some
small chapel where mass was said in the populous alley or forlorn
suburb?[29]

The appeal here is far more to the imagination than to the
intellect. It is, of course, obvious that Roman Catholicism is
lineally descended from primitive Christianity, but the point
for Newman is clinched by the imaginative realization that
modern Catholicism is "the nearest . . . to say the least, to the
religious sentiment, and what is called *ethos*, of the early
Church, nay, to that of the Apostles and Prophets . . . [who
were] saintly and heroic men . . . more like a Dominican
preacher, or a Jesuit missionary, or a Carmelite friar, more
like St. Toribio, or St. Vincent Ferrer, or St. Francis Xavier,
or St. Alphonso Liguori, than to any individuals, or to any
classes of men, that can be found in other communions."[30]
There are several highly rhetorical passages identifying the
early with the contemporary Roman Catholic Church, of
which this one is the most dramatic and the most explicit:

If then there is now a form of Christianity such, that it extends
throughout the world, though with varying measures of promi-
nence or prosperity in separate places;—that it lies under the
power of sovereigns and magistrates, in various ways alien to its
faith;—that flourishing nations and great empires, professing or
tolerating the Christian name, lie over against it as antago-
nists;—that schools of philosophy and learning are supporting

theories, and following out conclusions, hostile to it, and establishing an exegetical system subversive of its Scriptures;—that it has lost whole Churches by schism, and is now opposed by powerful communions once part of itself; that it has been altogether or almost driven from some countries;—that in others its line of teachers is overlaid, its flocks oppressed, its Churches occupied, its property held by what may be called a duplicate succession; that in others its members are degenerate and corrupt, and are surpassed in conscientiousness and in virtue, as in gifts of intellect, by the very heretics whom it condemns, that heresies are rife and bishops negligent within its own pale;—and that amid its disorders and fears there is but one Voice for whose decisions the peoples wait with trust, one Name and one See to which they look with hope, and that name Peter, and that see Rome;— such a religion is not unlike the Christianity of the fifth and sixth Centuries.[31]

The reader is invited to "see" the resemblance and to recognize the nineteenth-century Church of Rome as the Church of the apostles and martyrs. This is apologetic writing with a special emphasis on the imagination. Nor should it cause surprise when we think of Newman's own conversion. We recall how in the fateful summer vacation of 1839 as he was reading about the Monophysite controversy he experienced his first serious doubt about Anglicanism:

My stronghold was Antiquity; now here, in the middle of the fifth century, I found, as it seemed to me, Christendom of the sixteenth and the nineteenth centuries reflected. I saw my face in that mirror, and I was a Monophysite. The Church of the *Via Media* was in the position of the Oriental communion, Rome was, where she now is; and the Protestants were the Eutychians.[32]

A couple of months later Newman received another shock, although this time it struck his auditory rather than his visual imagination. His attention had been drawn to an article on the Donatist schism and its relevance to Anglicanism. At first, the intellectual force of the analogy did not at all impress Newman; the two ecclesial situations seemed quite different.

> But my friend ... pointed out the palmary words of St. Augustine, which were contained in one of the extracts made in the Review, and which had escaped my observation. "Securus judicat orbis terrarum." He kept repeating these words again and again, and, when he was gone, they kept ringing in my ears. "Securus judicat orbis terrarum"; they were words which went beyond the occasion of the Donatists: they applied to that of the Monophysites. . . . They decided ecclesiastical questions on a simpler rule than that of Antiquity; nay, St. Augustine was one of the prime oracles of Antiquity; here then Antiquity was deciding against itself. What a light was hereby thrown upon every controversy in the Church! . . .

The words which sounded so loudly in Newman's ears stimulated, of course, a series of intellectual reflections, but they also cast a new light on church history, placing old problems in a different, fresh perspective. This passage, one of the most powerful in all of his writings and worthy of that traumatic moment, concludes with an acknowledgement of the incalculable power of the imagination:

> Who can account for the impressions which are made on him? For a mere sentence, the words of St. Augustine, struck me with a power which I never had felt from any words before. To take a familiar instance, they were like the "Turn again Whittington" of the chime; or, to take a more serious one, they were like the "Tolle, lege,—Tolle, lege," of the child, which converted St. Augustine himself. "Securus judicat orbis terrarum!" By those great words of the ancient Father, interpreting and summing up the long and varied course of ecclesiastical history, the theory of the *Via Media* was absolutely pulverized.

It was true, Newman tells us, that "After a while, I got calm, and at length the vivid impression upon my imagination faded away," but still he "had seen the shadow of a hand upon the wall." However, although he now "determined to be guided, not by my imagination, but by my reason," this was not because he rejected the validity of the imagination, but because he knew that the mind consists of more than the imagination.[33] In his *Lectures on Certain Difficulties felt by Anglicans in submitting to the Catholic Church* (1850), Newman recounts how it was "the living picture" which the study of "history presents to us" that opened his eyes to the identity of the Church of the Fathers with the Roman Catholic Church. But this was only possible because of his ability to "see" the historical analogy: "That ancient history is not dead, it lives . . . we see ourselves in it, as in a glass, and if the *Via Media* was heretical then, it is heretical now." Naturally, it was impossible to prove an analogy like this to somebody else; it had to be "seen."[34]

The *Essay* may be more of an apologetic than a strictly systematic work, but it remains of great theological interest, not least because, as has been said, it is "the almost inevitable starting point for an investigation of development of doctrine."[35] However, it is also of great theological significance by virtue of its exemplifying the philosophy of the mind which Newman had adumbrated in the *Oxford University Sermons*. For it is not only the imagination which plays a crucial part in a theological inquiry, which Newman, as usual, sees as inseparable from the study of history. No less important is the concept of implicit as opposed to explicit knowledge. It has been claimed, for example, in a standard history of the theology of development that according to the *Essay* the original Christian revelation was given partly in feelings such as could hardly be developed into new doctrines which were not also an addition to revelation, since dogmatic propositions can hardly be deduced from wordless experiences.[36] Such criticism assumes that if the apostolic Church was not "conscious" of later dogmas, then she could not have been cognizant of them. But the problem disappears once we understand that Newman meant that the Church had an implicit but not an explicit knowledge of later doctrinal formulations. As he explained in the last of the *Oxford University Sermons*, "The Theory of Developments in Religious Doctrine," "It is no proof that persons are not possessed, because they are not conscious, of an idea."[37] Since he is not a systematic thinker or writer, Newman's terminology tends to be informal and there is no doubt that he occasionally does use the word "feelings," as in this sentence: "St. Justin or St. Irenaeus might be without any digested ideas of Purgatory or Original Sin, yet have an intense feeling, which they had not defined or located, both of the fault of our first nature and the responsibilities of our nature regenerate." But the immediately preceding sentence makes it perfectly clear that this feeling is not intended to be noncognitive: "the holy Apostles would without words know all the truths concerning the high doctrines of theology, which controversialists after them have piously and charitably reduced to formulae, and developed through argument."[38] What was implicitly believed becomes explicitly professed, as Newman expounds in the following passage which he quotes from the sermon on development, and which he introduces by commenting that in theology the mind develops "the solemn ideas, which it has hitherto held implicitly and without subjecting them to its reflecting and reasoning powers":

> The mind which is habituated to the thought of God, of Christ, of the Holy Spirit, naturally turns with a devout curiosity to the contemplation of the object of its adoration, and begins to form statements concerning it, before it knows whither, or how far, it will be carried. One proposition necessarily leads to another, and a second to a third; then some limitation is required; and the combination of these opposites occasions some fresh evolutions from the original idea, which indeed can never be said to be entirely exhausted. This process is its development, and results in a series, or rather body, of dogmatic statements, till what was an impression on the Imagination has become a system or creed in the Reason.

... As God is one, so the impression which He gives us of Himself is one.... It is the vision of an object.... Creeds and dogmas live in the one idea which they are designed to express, and which alone is substantive....[39]

The last paragraph shows how modern Newman's theology of revelation is in its "personalist" as opposed to "propositional" emphasis. But the whole passage surely makes it quite clear that Newman is concerned with an intuitive knowledge which is far more like "seeing" than "feeling."

Finally, any doubt is removed by a paper on doctrinal development Newman wrote in 1868 (in connexion with the controversy over papal infallibility), where he makes it plain that the "idea" the apostolic Church received was definitely known, although implicitly rather than explicitly:

the Apostles had the *fullness* of revealed knowledge, a fullness which they could as little realize to themselves, as the human mind, as such, can have all its thoughts present before it at once. They are elicited according to the occasion. A man of genius cannot go about with his genius in his hand: in an Apostle's mind great part of his knowledge is from the nature of the case latent or implicit....

Indeed, the "idea" which the Church has received is cognitive enough to be called a "Divine philosophy"—

not a number of formulas ... but a system of thought ... in such sense that a mind that was possessed of it, that is, the Church's mind, could definitely and unequivocally say whether this part of it, as traditionally expressed, meant this or that, and whether this or that was agreeable to, or inconsistent with it in whole or in part. I wish to hold that there is nothing which the Church has defined or shall define but what an Apostle, if asked, would have been fully able to answer and would have answered, as the Church has answered, the one answering by inspiration, the other from its gift of infallibility....

As an analogy, Newman cites the situation of someone who has complete knowledge of Aristotle's philosophy, and yet who cannot have "before his mind" every thought and saying of Aristotle, any more than Aristotle himself could have had "a host of thoughts present" to his mind "at once."

> The philosophy, as a system, is stored in the *memory* . . . and is brought out according to the occasion. A learned Aristotelian is one who can answer any whatever philosophical questions in the way that Aristotle would have answered them. If they are questions which could not occur in Aristotle's age, he still answers them . . . In one respect he knows more than Aristotle; because, in new emergencies after the time of Aristotle, he *can* and *does* answer what Aristotle would have answered, but for the want of the opportunity did not. There is another point of view in which he seems to have the advantage of Aristotle, though it is no real superiority, viz that, from the necessities of the interval between Aristotle and himself, there has been the growth of . . . a scientific vocabulary, which makes the philosophy easier to remember, easier to communicate and to defend. . . .

So, for example, St. Paul could hardly have understood what was meant by the "Immaculate Conception," but "if he had been asked, whether or not our Lady had the grace of the Spirit anticipating all sin whatever, including Adam's imputed sin, I think he would have answered in the affirmative." The "living idea," then, of Christianity, or what Newman as a Roman Catholic calls "the deposit of faith,"

> is in such sense committed to the Church or to the Pope, that when the Pope sits in St. Peter's chair, or when a Council of Fathers and doctors is collected round him, it is capable of being presented to their minds with that fullness and exactness . . . with which it habitually, not occasionally, resided in the minds of the Apostles;—a vision of it, not logical, and therefore consistent with errors of reasoning and of fact in the enunciation, after the manner of an intuition or an instinct.[40]

II

After he became a Catholic, Newman repeatedly repudiated any suggestion that he was a theologian or that he was qualified to write on theological subjects. Compared with his profound knowledge of Scripture and the Fathers, his familiarity with St. Thomas Aquinas and the Scholastic tradition was much more modest. And yet, more through force of circumstances than deliberate choice on his part, he was gradually led to develop an ecclesiology which in important ways anticipates the great Constitution on the Church of the Second Vatican Council and which remains highly relevant to some of the most sensitive theological problems of the postconciliar Church.

It was not until 1859, fourteen years after his conversion, that an attack by a seminary professor on a passage Newman had written in the liberal Catholic magazine, the *Rambler*, of which he had reluctantly become the editor, drew from him his first theological writing as a Catholic. Newman had dared to suggest that the bishops should ask the laity's opinion on educational matters, particularly since they had been "consulted" before the recent definition of the doctrine of the Immaculate Conception. He now defended himself by saying:

> To the unlearned reader the idea conveyed by "consulting" is not necessarily that of asking an opinion. For instance, we speak of consulting a barometer about the weather. The barometer does not give us its opinion, but ascertains for us a fact . . . I had not a dream of understanding the word . . . in the sense of *asking an opinion.*[41]

In conversation with his bishop, who was concerned about the offending passage, Newman remarked, with characteristic pragmatism, that "the Church would look foolish" without the laity.[42] Before resigning his editorship on the bishop's advice, he decided to deal more fully with the place of the laity in the Church. The result was the famous article "On Consulting the Faithful in Matters of Doctrine."

He begins by again defending his use of the word *consult*, which he says in ordinary English "includes the idea of inquiring into a matter of *fact*, as well as asking a judgment." Thus, for example, a "physician consults the pulse of his patient; but not in the same sense in which his patient consults *him.*" It is in the former sense that the Church "consults" or "regards" the faith of the laity before defining a doctrine. For, although the laity's "advice, their opinion, their judgment on the question of definition is not asked," nevertheless, "the matter of fact, viz. their belief, *is* sought for, as a testimony to that apostolical tradition, on which alone any doctrine whatsoever can be defined."[43] The laity is consulted "because the body of the faithful is one of the witnesses to the fact of the tradition of revealed doctrine, and because their *consensus* through Christendom is the voice of the Infallible Church." There are "channels of tradition," through which "the tradition of the Apostles, committed to the whole Church . . . manifests itself variously at various times," none of which "may be treated with disrespect," even though the hierarchy has sole responsibility for "discerning, discriminating, defining, promulgating, and enforcing any portion of that tradition."[44] He himself, he explains, is "accustomed to lay great stress on the *consensus fidelium*" in order to compensate for the lack of testimony from bishops and theologians in favor of defined points of doctrine. At the time of the definition of the Immaculate Conception, Bishop Ullathorne had referred to the faith of the laity as a "reflection" of the teaching of the Church, and Newman comments with dry irony: "Reflection; that is, the people are a *mirror*, in which the Bishops see themselves. Well, I suppose a person may *consult* his glass, and in that way may know things about himself which he can learn in no other way."[45]

He now proceeds to his celebrated historical example drawn from that period of the early Church's history which he had studied so deeply and intensely as an Anglican. In spite of the fact that the fourth century was the age of great doctors and saints, who were also bishops, like Athanasius, Ambrose, Chrysostom, and Augustine, "nevertheless in that very day the divine tradition committed to the infallible Church was proclaimed and maintained far more by the faithful than by the Episcopate." During the Arian heresy, "in that time of immense confusion the divine dogma of our Lord's divinity was proclaimed, enforced, maintained, and (humanly speaking) preserved, far more by the 'Ecclesia docta' than by the 'Ecclesia docens' . . . the body of the episcopate was unfaithful to its commission, while the body of the laity was faithful to its baptism." The importance of the illustration is shown by the fact that it occurred so early in the history of the Church and involved the very identity of Christ. Newman boldly concludes by saying that "there was a temporary suspense of the functions" of the teaching Church, the unpalatable truth being that the "body of Bishops failed in their confession of the faith." The danger of the present time, when the hierarchy was so faithful and orthodox, was that the role of the laity would be neglected—but "each constituent portion of the Church has its proper functions, and no portion can safely be neglected." The article ends with an almost defiant challenge, in the well-known words:

> I think certainly that the Ecclesia docens is more happy when she has . . . enthusiastic partisans about her . . . than when she cuts off the faithful from the study of her divine doctrines . . . and requires from them a fides implicita in her word, which in the educated classes will terminate in indifference, and in the poorer in superstition.[46]

A controversial issue had elicited from Newman his first contribution to theology as a Catholic. His next major essay in ecclesiology was also the fruit of controversy—this time not with Catholics but with an Anglican critic, Charles Kingsley. However, the writing in question, which takes up a major part of the fifth and last chapter of the Apologia pro Vita Sua, is directed only ostensibly at Kingsley, for in reality it is aimed chiefly at two opposing groups of his co-religionists, the liberal Catholics and (especially) the Ultramontanes.[47]

Defending the Catholic belief in the Church's infallibility,

Newman calls it a "power . . . happily adapted to be a working instrument . . . for smiting hard and throwing back the immense energy of the aggressive, capricious, untrustworthy intellect." There follows a severely uncompromising exposition of the Church's authority "viewed in its fulness" and "viewed in the concrete, as clothed and surrounded by the appendages of its high sovereignty . . . a supereminent prodigious power sent upon earth to encounter and master a giant evil." Although infallibility strictly only belongs to solemn dogmatic definitions, Newman professes to submit not only to the traditions of the Church, but also "to those other decisions of the Holy See, theological or not . . . which, waiving the question of their infallibility, on the lowest ground come to me with a claim to be accepted and obeyed." Nor does he feel any "temptation at all to break in pieces the great legacy of thought" which the Church has inherited from her greatest thinkers.[48]

This unequivocal statement provokes the obvious objection that "the restless intellect of our common humanity is utterly weighed down" by such an authority, "so that, if this is to be the mode of bringing it into order, it is brought into order only to be destroyed." This leads to the claim that in fact the "energy of the human intellect . . . thrives and is joyous, with a tough elastic strength, under the terrible blows of the divinely-fashioned weapon, and is never so much itself as when it has lately been overthrown." The resolution of the conflict lies in the remarkable argument that, far from being mutually contradictory, authority and reason need each other precisely because, paradoxically, each is actually sustained by conflict with the other:

> it is the vast Catholic body itself, and it only, which affords an arena for both combatants in that awful, never-dying duel. It is necessary for the very life of religion . . . that the warfare should be incessantly carried on. Every exercise of Infallibility is brought out into act by an intense and varied operation of the Reason, both as its ally and as its opponent, and provokes again, when it has done its work, a re-action of Reason against it; and, as in

a civil polity the State exists and endures by means of the rivalry and collision, the encroachments and defeats of its constituent parts, so in like manner Catholic Christendom is no simple exhibition of religious absolutism, but presents a continuous picture of Authority and Private Judgment alternately advancing and retreating as the ebb and flow of the tide;—it is a vast assemblage of human beings with wilful intellects and wild passions, brought together into one by the beauty and the Majesty of a Superhuman Power,—into what may be called a large reformatory or training-school, not as if into a hospital or into a prison, not in order to be sent to bed, not to be buried alive, but (if I may change my metaphor) brought together as if into some moral factory, for the melting, refining, and moulding, by an incessant, noisy process, of the raw material of human nature, so excellent, so dangerous, so capable of divine purpose.[49]

The infallible authority, Newman insists, "is a supply for a need, and it does not go beyond that need," for its purpose is "not to enfeeble the freedom or vigour of human thought in religious speculation, but to resist and control its extravagance." Having begun by freely admitting the wide powers enjoyed by ecclesiastical authority, he now emphasizes both the narrow limits of infallibility in defining as explicit doctrine what is already implicit in revelation, and also its rare occurrence (normally by a "Pope in Ecumenical Council"). But, more important, he recognizes what "*is* the great trial to the Reason," namely, that the Church claims jurisdiction over a wide area of "secular matters which bear upon religion." These disciplinary rather than doctrinal judgments are not, however, infallible—but they do claim obedience (although not faith). Again, "because there is a gift of infallibility in the Catholic Church," it does not necessarily follow that "the parties who are in possession of it are in all their proceedings infallible." Indeed, "I think history supplies us with instances in the Church, where legitimate power has been harshly used." The unequivocal assertion of the Church's legitimate authority is thus sharply qualified by these reminders of its limits and limitations. But the apparent discrepancy is resolved by the consideration that it does not "follow that the substance of the acts of the ruling power is not right and expedient, because its manner may have been faulty." In fact, Newman remarks tartly, "high authorities act by means of instruments," and "we know how such instruments claim for themselves the name of their principals, who thus get the credit of faults which really are not theirs."[50]

The pages that follow are probably unrivaled in Newman's works for their sharply antithetical style of argument, brilliantly deployed to hold a carefully poised balance between two diametrically opposed points of view. But the object is not to play a balancing-trick between liberal Catholics on the one side and Ultramontanes on the other. Nor is the pattern of thought no more than a rhetorical device designed to reach a compromise between the claims of both parties. For what emerges is that truth is attained not in spite of but through the conflict of opposites, which forces the crucial shift of perspective that allows the dilemma to be seen in a new light and so to be resolved.

Newman begins by reinforcing the case for authority and the need for submission. Even Protestants "have before now obeyed the royal command to abstain from certain theological questions." Moreover, despite all abuses, Newman insists that ecclesiastical authority has been "mainly in the right, and that those whom they were hard upon were mainly in the wrong." For example, Origen (whose name "I love") "was wrong" and "his opponents were right." And yet—"who can speak with patience of his enemy and the enemy of St. John Chrysostom, that Theophilus, bishop of Alexandria? who can admire or revere Pope Vigilius?" The contradiction is resolved by a completely fresh perspective, at once enlightening and provocative:

> In reading ecclesiastical history, when I was an Anglican, it used to be forcibly brought home to me, how the initial error of what afterwards became heresy was the urging forward some truth

against the prohibition of authority at an unseasonable time. There is a time for every thing, and many a man desires a reformation of an abuse, or the fuller development of a doctrine, or the adoption of a particular policy, but forgets to ask himself whether the right time for it is come: and knowing that there is no one who will be doing any thing towards its accomplishment in his own lifetime unless he does it himself, he will not listen to the voice of authority, and he spoils a good work in his own century, in order that another man, as yet unborn, may not have the opportunity of bringing it happily to perfection in the next. He may seem to the world to be nothing else than a bold champion for the truth and a martyr to free opinion, when he is just one of those persons whom the competent authority ought to silence; and, though the case may not fall within that subject-matter in which that authority is infallible, or the formal conditions of the exercise of that gift may be wanting, it is clearly the duty of authority to act vigorously in the case.

This, Newman admits, will arouse criticism, especially "if the ruling power happens in its proceedings to evince any defect of prudence or consideration." Mindful, no doubt, of his own difficulties with liberal Catholics who disliked his insistence on obedience, Newman adds that "all those who take the part of that ruling authority will be considered as time-savers, or indifferent to the cause of uprightness and truth." But that is not the conclusion of the sentence. The surprise, or rather the sting, lies in the second half, directed not at the liberals, but at the Ultramontanes: "while, on the other hand, the said authority may be accidentally supported by a violent ultra party, which exalts opinions into dogmas, and has it principally at heart to destroy every school of thought but its own."[51]

However, Newman argues, the proof that infallibility has not crushed intellectual freedom in the Church is that it is "individuals, and not the Holy See, that have taken the initiative, and given the lead to the Catholic mind, in theological inquiry." "Indeed," he points out with studied irony, "it is one

of the reproaches against the Roman Church, that it has
originated nothing, and has only served as a sort of *remora* or
break in the development of doctrine. And it is an objection
which I really embrace as a truth; for such I conceive to be
the main purpose of its extraordinary gift." The historical
examples that follow are unrelentingly negative. The fact is
that "the Church of Rome possessed no great mind in the
whole period of persecution." There was not a single doctor
till St. Leo, who anyway taught only "one point of doctrine."
Not even Pope St. Gregory has a place in the history of
theology. The greatest Western theologian, St. Augustine,
belonged, like the best early Latin theologians, to the African
Church. Western theology, in fact, was formed to a considerable extent by heterodox theologians such as Tertullian and
Origen and Eusebius, with the result that actual heretical
"questionings" became "salutary truths." Even ecumenical
councils were guided by the "individual reason" of a mere
presbyter like Malchion, or a young deacon like Athanasius.
At Trent, too, particular theologians "had a critical effect on
some of the definitions of dogma." The real, albeit hidden,
conclusion is that history gives little support to the Ultramon-
tane view of Rome as a kind of oracle of truth.[52]

History, too, shows how little authority has interfered with
the freedom of theologians. Again, beneath the apparent
movement of the argument, there runs a contrary, stronger
undercurrent, for what really concerns Newman, of course, is
that what was true of the past is no longer true of the present.
But he is not only protesting against the present by means of
the past; he is also stating with great deliberateness his considered view on the crucial balance to be maintained between
theology and the teaching authority of the Church. He begins
by referring (provocatively) to that theocratic society so idealized by many of his fellow converts.

There never was a time when the intellect of the educated class
was more active, or rather more restless, than in the middle ages.
And then again all through Church history from the first, how

slow is authority in interfering! Perhaps a local teacher, or a doctor in some local school, hazards a proposition, and a controversy ensues. It smoulders or burns in one place, no one interposing; Rome simply lets it alone. Then it comes before a Bishop; or some priest, or some professor in some other seat of learning takes it up; and then there is a second stage of it. Then it comes before a University, and it may be condemned by the theological faculty. So the controversy proceeds year after year, and Rome is still silent. An appeal perhaps is next made to a seat of authority inferior to Rome; and then at last after a long while it comes before the supreme power. Meanwhile, the question has been ventilated and turned over and over again, and viewed on every side of it, and authority is called upon to pronounce a decision, which has already been arrived at by reason. But even then, perhaps the supreme authority hesitates to do so, and nothing is determined on the point for years; or so generally and vaguely, that the whole controversy has to be gone through again, before it is ultimately determined.

Newman, even at this point, when his own personal interest is almost palpable, refrains from outright criticism of the abuse of authority in the contemporary Church. But the rhetoric of reticence has its own eloquence:

It is manifest how a mode of proceeding, such as this, tends not only to the liberty, but to the courage, of the individual theologian or controversialist. Many a man has ideas, which he hopes are true, and useful for his day, but he is not confident about them, and wishes to have them discussed. He is willing, or rather would be thankful, to give them up, if they can be proved to be erroneous or dangerous, and by means of controversy he achieves his end. He is answered, and he yields; or on the contrary he finds that he is considered safe. He would not dare to do this, if he knew an authority, which was supreme and final, was watching every word he said, and made signs of assent or dissent to each sentence, as he uttered it. Then indeed he would be fighting, as the Persian soldiers, under the lash, and the freedom of his intellect might truly be said to be beaten out of him.

Typically, even now he is ready to undermine his own indignation with the frank qualification that "when controversies run high" then "an interposition may . . . advisably take place; and again, questions may be of that urgent nature, that an appeal must, as a matter of duty, be made at once to the highest authority in the Church." But the insistent emphasis on the universal character of the Church that follows barely conceals an unfavorable allusion to the Italian monopoly of the Holy See.

> [T]he multitude of nations which are within the fold of the Church will be found to have acted for its protection, against any narrowness, on the supposition of narrowness, in the various authorities at Rome, with whom lies the practical decision of controverted questions. . . . Then, again, such national influences have a providential effect in moderating the bias which the local influences of Italy may exert on the See of St. Peter. It stands to reason that . . . Rome must have in it an element of Italy; and it is no prejudice to the zeal and devotion with which we submit ourselves to the Holy See to admit this plainly . . . Catholicity is not only one of the notes of the Church, but . . . one of its securities.

And the conclusion is daringly ambiguous, if not sarcastic:

> I trust that all European races will ever have a place in the Church, and assuredly I think that the loss of the English, not to say the German element, in its composition has been a most serious misfortune. And certainly, if there is one consideration more than another which should make us English grateful to Pius the Ninth, it is that, by giving us a Church of our own, he has prepared the way for our own habits of mind, our own manner of reasoning, our own tastes, and our own virtues, finding a place and thereby a sanctification, in the Catholic Church.[53]

What emerges from these last pages of the *Apologia* is not, of course, anything in the nature of a systematic theology of the magisterium. But then, the implication of the argument is that there is an important sense in which it is inappropriate

to seek any kind of blueprint for the relation between authority and freedom in the Church. The point of Newman's carefully balanced dialectic is that it is impossible either to describe or to prescribe exactly how this aspect of the Church's
life is lived or ought to be lived. No theory can cover every
concrete situation, which has to be judged pragmatically in
every case. What can be done is to set out some guidelines:
first, to stress the importance of both authority and freedom;
second, to emphasize the creative value of an interaction
which inevitably involves tension; third, to modify and qual-
ify the legitimate claims of authority; fourth, to show how it
is precisely conflict which may force open the new perspective
that allows the resolution of a difficulty; fifth, to distinguish
carefully between the theological and magisterial offices in the
Church; sixth, to suggest practical ways in which justice may
be done to the rights of both the magisterium and the theologians; and, finally, to plead for that catholicity of the Church
that gives due recognition to local national churches but without prejudice to the ultimate jurisdiction of Rome.

The most important theological work from the ecumenical
point of view that Newman wrote as a Catholic is his *Letter
to Pusey* (1866). It was written ostensibly in reply to E. B.
Pusey's so-called *Eirenicon*, which dealt severely with Roman
Catholic mariology, but again it was also an opportunity for
Newman to launch a counterattack on the dominant Ultra-
montane party.

As an early ecumenist, Newman prefers to minimize religious differences, not by attempting to find a lowest common
denominator, but rather by looking behind the apparently
irreconcilable positions to see how far they are real and how
far merely verbal. Pusey had implied that Rome denied that
"the whole Christian faith is contained in Scripture," but
Newman boldly maintains that the difference between Anglicans and Catholics "is merely one of words," depending on
what is meant by "proof": "We mean that not every article of
faith is so contained there, that it may thence be logically
proved, *independently* of the teaching and authority of the

Tradition; but Anglicans mean that every article of faith is so contained there, that it may thence be proved, *provided* there be added the illustrations and compensations supplied by the Tradition."[54] If there was only really a verbal disagreement, then genuine agreement could be reached on this particular vexed theological issue.

Pusey's remarks about the duty of converts to accept the religious system of their adopted church provide Newman with his opening, as he proceeds to explain his motive and purpose in writing. On the one hand, he readily accepts that a convert "comes to Catholicism as to a living system, with a living teaching, and not to a mere collection of decrees and canons," while to embrace only "the framework, not the body and substance of the Church" would "not only be unreal, but would be dangerous, too, as arguing a wrong state of mind." On the other hand, by "not risking the loss of revealed truth altogether by attempting by a private rule to discriminate every moment its substance from its accidents," the convert "is gradually so indoctrinated in Catholicism, as at length to have a right to speak as well as to hear." He becomes aware of "the fact and the nature of the differences of theologian from theologian, school from school, nation from nation, era from era" and that "there is much of what may be called fashion in opinions and practices"—and, Newman adds significantly, "that fashions change." Not only that, but he even discovers that "sometimes what is denounced in one place as a great offence, or preached up as a first principle, has in another nation been immemorially regarded in just a contrary sense." With his tongue somewhat in his cheek, Newman remarks that it may actually be "disloyal" to the Church authorities not to make known one's views, when they need to know all sides of the question before coming to a decision. Given these differences, he feels "no delicacy" in stating frankly that "I prefer English habits of belief and devotion to foreign." And he adds, "In following those of my people, I show less singularity, and create less disturbance than if I made a flourish with what is novel and exotic."[55]

So far as Newman is concerned, the essential Marian doc-trines are all to be found in antiquity: devotion to Mary has increased, but there has been no "growth" in doctrine, for "it has been in substance one and the same from beginning."[56]

> The sun in the spring-time will have to shine many days before he is able to melt the frost, open the soil, and bring out the leaves; yet he shines out from the first notwithstanding, though he makes his power felt but gradually. It is one and the same sun, though his influence day by day becomes greater; and so in the Catholic Church it is the one Virgin Mother, one and the same from first to last, and Catholics may have ever acknowl-edged her; and yet, in spite of that acknowledgement, their devotion to her may be scanty in one time and place, and over-flowing in another.

Far from Italianate devotions being obligatory for English Catholics, the "distinction is forcibly brought home to a con-vert, as a peculiarity of the Catholic religion," that while the "faith is everywhere one and the same," nevertheless, "a large liberty is accorded to private judgment and inclination as regards matters of devotion."[57] And far from devotional prac-tices having any kind of absolute character, Newman empha-sizes that in fact they vary a lot from age to age, some declin-ing, others arising.

His exposition of the Catholic teaching about Mary begins with the Fathers' view of her as the "Second Eve." This he had already explained in his *Essay on the Development of Chris-tian Doctrine*, from which "the greater part" of the pamphlet was taken—"I have done little more than throw it into a more popular form."[58] The most important and original part of the *Letter to Pusey* is, not surprisingly, the last part, where New-man turns to discuss the devotions as opposed to the beliefs of Catholics. He begins by pointing out that ordinary people would find it hard to distinguish logically between the patristic view of Mary held by Pusey and the modern Catholic views he criticizes. Granted that there are real distinctions, still, it is very hard to draw the line exactly—a consideration which stimulates a particularly eloquent passage expressive of one of Newman's deepest insights into the nature of life, and one of ecclesiological significance which tells as much against Pusey as against the Ultramontanes.

It is impossible, I say, in a doctrine like this, to draw the line clearly between truth and error, right and wrong. This is ever the case in concrete matters, which have life. Life in this world is motion, and involves a continual process of change. Living things grow into their perfection, into their decline, into their death. No rule of art will suffice to stop the operation of this natural law, whether in the material world or in the human mind. We can indeed encounter disorders, when they occur, by external antagonism and remedies; but we cannot eradicate the process itself, out of which they arise. Life has the same right to decay, as it has to wax strong. This is specially the case with great ideas. You may stifle them; or you may refuse them elbow-room; or again you may torment them with your continuing meddling; or you may let them have free course and range, and be content, instead of anticipating their excesses, to expose and restrain those excesses after they have occurred. But you have only this alternative; and for myself, I prefer much wherever it is possible, to be first generous and then just; to grant full liberty of thought, and to call it to account when abused.

And Newman concludes specifically: "If what I have been saying be true of energetic ideas generally, much more is it the case in matters of religion. Religion acts on the affections; who is to hinder these, when once roused, from gathering in their strength and running wild?"[59]

Taking ordinary human love as an analogy, Newman argues that religious devotion which "is abstractedly extravagant, may in particular persons be becoming and beautiful, and only fall under blame when it is found in others who imitate them. When it is formalized into meditations or exercises, it is as repulsive as love-letters in a police report."[60] He now proceeds to make a more generalized observation which in itself represents a further stage in his developing theology of the

Church—and one which also provides a key to one enigmatic aspect of Catholicism:

> the religion of the multitude is ever vulgar and abnormal; it ever will be tinctured with fanaticism and superstition, while men are what they are. A people's religion is ever a corrupt religion, in spite of the provisions of Holy Church. . . . You may beat religion out of men, if you will, and then their excesses will take a different direction; but if you make use of religion to improve them, they will make use of religion to corrupt it. And then you will have effected that compromise of which our countrymen report so unfavourably from abroad—a high grand faith and worship which compels their admiration, and puerile absurdities among the people which excite their contempt.[61]

As he explained once in a letter, "a popular religion is necessarily deformed by the errors and bad taste of the multitude," for "the religion of a nation will ever partake of the peculiar faults of the national character": "The most sublime truths take a vulgar shape and bear a forbidding aspect, when reflected back by the masses of human society—nay, often cannot be made intelligible to them, or at least cannot be made to reach them, till thrown into words or actions which are offensive to educated minds." Disapprove as the Church may, "she may find it quite impossible to root out the tares without rooting out the wheat with them."[62]

Newman's developed ecclesiology includes a theology of the corruption of the Church not simply for apologetic purposes, but because corruption is seen as inseparable from a living Church—"things that do not admit of abuse have very little life in them."[63] As he was to explain a few years later, "since the world is ever corrupt, therefore when it has poured into the Church, it has insulted and blasphemed the religion which it professed, in a special way, in which heathenism cannot insult it. I *grant* that a Protestant world cannot commit that sin which a Catholic world can. . . . " It is when ordinary human weaknesses are "coupled with that intense absolute faith which Catholics have, and Protestants have not," that one finds "acts of inconsistency, of superstition, violence, etc., which are not to be looked for external to the Catholic Church."[64] It was impossible to think of a time when "the greatest scandals did not exist in the Church, and act as impediments to the success of its mission," scandals which had been "the occasion of momentous secessions and schisms." But in spite of these scandals, "the Church has ever got on and made way, to the surprise of the world; as an army may fight a series of bloody battles, and lose men, and yet go forward from victory to victory." The "seceding bodies," on the other hand, "have sooner or later come to nought"—"At this very time we are witnessing the beginning of the end of Protestantism, the breaking of that bubble of 'Bible-Christianity' which has been its life." Not only had Jesus Christ predicted scandals, but he had spoken of his Church "as in its very constitution made up of good and bad." The corruption of the Church had existed from the time of Judas Iscariot, and was "bound up with the very idea of Christianity," and was "almost a dogma."[65]

As for distortions and exaggerations in Marian devotions, Newman notes that it is those countries that "have lost their faith in the divinity of Christ, who have given up devotion to His Mother," while "those on the other hand, who had been foremost in her honour, have retained their orthodoxy." "In the Catholic Church," Newman insists, "Mary has shown herself, not the rival, but the minister of her Son; she has protected Him, as in his infancy, so in the whole history of the Religion."[66] The corruption of this vitality lies in certain "extravagances"—from which, Newman dares to say, "I suppose we owe it to the national good sense, that English Catholics have been protected." It is these "curiosities of thought," he remarks severely, "which are both so attractive to undisciplined imaginations and so dangerous to grovelling hearts."[67] While it would be "a simple purism" to "insist upon minute accuracy of expression in devotional and popular writings"— as though "we . . . disparage Divine Providence when we say that we are indebted to our parents for our life"—nevertheless,

Newman admits that a few of Pusey's quotations from foreign
devotional writers "affected me with grief and almost anger."
Still, what appeared like idolatry might be justifiable in certain contexts or senses. Where there have clearly been excesses, but where it is "not easy to convict them of definite
error logically," then it may be hard for authority to take
action, as in a court of law "when the commission of an
offence is morally certain, but the government prosecutor cannot find legal evidence sufficient to insure conviction."[68]
However, he insists that Marian "intercession is one thing,
devotion is another"—and they must not be confused (implicitly, either by Pusey or extreme Catholic writers). Otherwise,
"there would be grave reasons for doubting of the salvation of
St. Chrysostom or St. Athanasius"; indeed, he wonders
"whether St. Augustine, in all his voluminous writings, in-
vokes her once." But none of this alters the fact that Mary
"intercedes for those Christians who do not know her."[69]

The conclusion is typically even-handed. On the one
hand, some of Pusey's quotations "seem to me like a bad
dream" and, in the English context at any rate, "calculated
to prejudice inquirers, to frighten the unlearned, to unsettle
consciences, to provoke blasphemy, and to work the loss of
souls." On the other hand, Pusey himself is not spared, because paradoxically his own work points in the same direction:

> Have you not been teaching us on a very tender point in a very
> rude way? is it not the effect of what you have said to expose her
> to scorn and obloquy, who is dearer to us than any other crea-
> ture? Have you even hinted that our love for her is anything else
> than an abuse? Have you thrown her one kind word yourself all
> through your book?[70]

Newman's next "pamphlet"—actually again a short book
in length—is his A Letter to the Duke of Norfolk (1875), where
once more he tries to steer a middle course between the two
extreme positions on the question of papal infallibility. In
dissociating himself both from the Ultramontanes and from
the irreconcilable opponents of the Vatican Council defini-

tion, he adds a new important consideration to the general point he had made in the *Apologia* about the interdependence of the magisterium and theology. He also shows, as in his earliest Anglican theological writing, his concern to avoid confusing orthodoxy with fundamentalism. At the very beginning of the *Letter* he emphasizes a point he had already made with some force, before the definition, in a letter of March 1870, where he pointed out that even the pronouncements of an infallible pope would still require interpretation. The same was true of a council's definitions, which—just as "lawyers explain acts of Parliament"—had to be explained by theologians. Obvious as the fact might be, the conclusion to be drawn from it had serious consequences for the fantasies of extreme Ultramontanism. "Hence, I have never been able to see myself that the ultimate decision rests with any but the general Catholic intelligence." Such a realistic theology of "reception" was simply a further implication of Newman's cherished maxim, "Securus judicat orbis terrarum" (which Newman freely translated as "The universal Church is in its judgments secure of truth").[71] In the *Letter to the Duke of Norfolk*, he was careful to emphasize the fact that the whole Church had to ratify a definition as "authentic," did not mean that the "subsequent reception" actually entered into the "necessary conditions" of a dogmatic decision.[72] In the earlier private letter he also noted that abstract definitions could not "determine particular fact": the doctrine, for example, that there was no salvation outside the Church did not apply to people in "invincible ignorance."[73] For "it does not follow, because there is no Church but one, which has the Evangelical gifts and privileges to bestow, that therefore no one can be saved without the intervention of that one Church." And it was "possible to belong to the soul of the Church without belonging to the body."[74]

Other teachings of the Church admitted of exceptions in practice, like the condemnations in theory of mixed education and usury. In the case of usury, moreover, as in that of the doctrine of absolute predestination, distinctions had been drawn between different connotations of the words in question, which had led to the serious modification, even suspension, of the abstract teaching. Such changes and qualifications in the Church's official teaching "show what caution is to be observed" in interpreting her pronouncements.[75] But, on the other hand, because general doctrines cannot be divorced from concrete circumstances and contexts, it did not follow that condemnations of "the very wording" of particular doctrinal deviations in books may not be infallible, since otherwise "neither Pope nor Council could draw up a dogmatic definition at all, for the right exercise of words is involved in the right exercise of thought."[76]

He continued to insist after the definition of papal infallibility that "the voice of the Schola Theologorum, of the whole Church diffusive" would "in time make itself heard," and that "Catholic instincts and ideas" would eventually "assimilate and harmonize" it into the wider context of Catholic belief.[77] As time went on, too, theologians would "settle the force of the wording of the dogma, just as the courts of law solve the meaning and bearing of Acts of Parliament."[78] While it was hardly more than common sense that ultimately the only way in which the solemn declarations of councils and popes could be authenticated was by the acceptance and recognition by the Church that they were indeed what they purported to be, nevertheless their interpretation involved necessarily the technicalities of theological science: the meaning of dogmatic statements was not self-evident, but they were "always made with the anticipation and condition of this lawyer-like, or special-pleader-like, action of the intellect upon them."[79] All human statements required interpretation. In defining doctrines, popes and councils enjoyed an "active infallibility," but more was involved in the infallibility of the Church than that, since a *passive infallibility* belonged to the whole Catholic people, who had to determine the force and meaning of these doctrinal definitions, although the chief responsibility for this lay with the theologians, whose discussions and investigations assured a clear distinction between "theological truth" and "theological opinion," which was essential for preventing "dogmatism." The differences between theologians maintained "liberty of thought," whilst their consensus on points of dogma was "the safeguard of the infallible decisions of the Church."[80] Infallibility (itself a comparatively recent term) resided in its fullness in the whole Church (although this had always been assumed and never formally defined)—*securus judicat orbis terrarum*.

In his treatment of the role of theology, Newman repeats and develops the points he had already made in private correspondence. He does not hesitate to say that the "definite rules" and "traditional principles of interpretation" needed for interpreting dogmatic statements are "as cogent and unchangeable" as the definitions themselves.[81] Central to this process, he claims, is the "principle of minimizing,"[82] whereby theologians explain "in the concrete" a pronouncement of the teaching authority, "by strict interpretation of its wording, by the illustration of its circumstances, and by the recognition of exceptions, in order to make it as tolerable as possible, and the least of a temptation, to self-willed, independent, or wrongly educated minds." After all, he insists, the virtue of faith is "so difficult," and "so difficult is it to assent inwardly to propositions, verified to us neither by reason nor experience, but depending for their reception on the word of the Church as God's oracle, that she has ever shown the utmost care to contract, as far as possible, the range of truths and the sense of propositions, of which she demands this absolute reception.[83] This "legitimate minimizing" takes advantage, on the one hand, of the "intensely concrete character of the matters condemned" in "negative" pronouncements and, on the other hand, of the abstract nature of "affirmative" definitions of doctrine ("excepting such as relate to persons"), which "admit of exceptions in their actual application."[84] These principles have to be applied to the definition of papal

infallibility, the scope of which is carefully limited to deliberate and actual definitions of faith and morals, which are refer-
able either to revelation or to the moral law, and which are
intended to be authoritative teachings, binding on the whole
Church as pertaining to salvation. In the event, however, of
"a false interpretation" of the infallibility definition, then "another Leo will be given us for the occasion." The reference is
to Pope St. Leo's Council of Chalcedon, which, "without of
course touching the definition" of the preceding Council of
Ephesus, "trimmed the balance of doctrine by completing
it."[85] The warning is an exact prophecy both of the theology
of "creeping infallibility" that came in the wake of the First
Vatican Council and of the Second Vatican Council, which
Pope John XXIII convoked nearly a hundred years later.

At the heart of A *Letter to the Duke of Norfolk* is the celebrated treatment of the sovereignty of conscience. Newman,
of course, had often written on conscience as the basis of
religious belief. But here he discusses the individual believer's
conscience in its relation to ecclesiastical authority. He first
defines conscience as the law of God "as apprehended in the
minds of individual men"—which, "though it may suffer refraction in passing into the intellectual medium of each . . .
is not therefore so affected as to lose its character of being the
Divine Law, but still has, as such, the prerogative of commanding obedience." On this view of conscience it is "the
voice of God," whereas the world regards it as little more than
"a creation of man." Far from being "a long-sighted selfish-
ness" or "a desire to be consistent with oneself," Newman
declares in ringing tones that "Conscience is the aboriginal
Vicar of Christ, a prophet in its informations, a monarch in
its peremptoriness, a priest in its blessings and anathemas,
and, even though the eternal priesthood throughout the
Church could cease to be, in it the sacerdotal principle would
remain and would have a sway." In earlier times "its supremacy was assailed by the arm of physical force," but "now the
intellect is put in operation to sap the foundations of a power

which the sword could not destroy." The threat is grandiloquently conveyed, but for all its fragile vulnerability, conscience has a strange, indestructible life:

> All through my day there has been a resolute warfare, I had almost said conspiracy against the rights of conscience, as I have described it. Literature and science have been embodied in great institutions in order to put it down. Noble buildings have been reared as fortresses against that spiritual, invisible influence which is too subtle for science and too profound for literature. Chairs in Universities have been made the seats of an antagonist tradition.

The secularized idea of conscience merely concerns "the right of thinking, speaking, writing, and acting" as one sees fit, "without any thought of God at all." Paradoxically, it has become "the very right and freedom of conscience to dispense with conscience." In effect, conscience "has been superseded by a counterfeit," namely, "the right of self-will."[86] Were the pope himself to "speak against Conscience in the true sense of the word, he would commit a suicidal act. He would be cutting the ground from under his feet." Indeed, continues Newman, "we shall find that it is by the universal sense of right and wrong, the consciousness of transgression, the pangs of guilt, and the dread of retribution, as first principles deeply lodged in the hearts of men, it is thus and only thus, that he has gained his footing in the world and achieved his success." It is the "championship of the Moral Law and of conscience" which is "his *raison d'etre*," and the "fact of his mission is the answer to the complaints of those who feel the insufficiency of the natural light; and the insufficiency of that light is the justification of his mission." Once again Newman emphasizes the precarious nature of the moral sense, which "is at once the highest of all teachers, yet the least luminous; and the Church, the Pope, the Hierarchy are . . . the supply of an urgent demand." But if revelation is the fulfilment of natural religion, it is in no sense "independent of it": "The Pope, who comes of Revelation, has no jurisdiction over Nature."[87]

Turning to the crucial question of the relation of the individual conscience to authority, Newman begins by laying down that since "conscience is not a judgment upon any speculative truth, any abstract doctrine, but bears immediately . . . on something to be done or not done," it "cannot come into direct collision with the Church's or the Pope's infallibility; which is engaged on general propositions, and in the condemnation of particular and given errors." Here Newman means by conscience not what moral theologians call "habitual" conscience, that is, the conscience which entertains general moral norms and principles, but rather what they mean by "actual" conscience, that is, the judgment that this particular thing here and now is to be done or not done (always, of course, in the light of the relevant moral principles). In other words, my "habitual" conscience on the one hand tells me that lying is wrong, but on the other hand my "actual" conscience has to decide whether this particular statement qualifies as a lie as opposed, for example, to an evasion, and also whether if it is a lie it is justifiable to prevent a greater evil. Or again, my "habitual" conscience may tell me that indiscriminate bombing is wrong but my "actual" conscience has to decide whether this particular bombing raid counts as an instance of indiscriminate bombing and, if so, whether the prevention of a greater evil may justify it. Even in the case of the most (apparently) unexceptionable moral rules, like, for example, "torturing innocent children is always wrong," the "actual" conscience has still to decide whether this particular action counts as torture or as justifiable punishment. And so, Newman argues, because "actual" conscience is "a practical dictate," *direct* conflict is possible "only when the Pope legislates, or gives particular orders, and the like." However, "a Pope is not infallible in his laws, nor in his commands, nor in his acts of state, nor in his administration, nor in his public policy." After all, St. Peter was not infallible at Antioch when St. Paul disagreed with him, nor was Liberius when he excommunicated Athanasius. However, the "dictate" of conscience, "in order to prevail against the voice of the Pope, must follow upon serious thought, prayer, and all available means of arriving at a right judgment on the matter in question." The onus of proof, then, lies on the individual conscience: "Unless a man is able to say to himself, as in the Presence of God, that he must not, and dare not, act upon the Papal injunction, he is bound to obey it, and would commit a great sin in disobeying it."[88] As usual, the bold admission about the fallibility of the first pope in no way excludes a rigorous emphasis on loyalty and obedience to a legitimate superior. But on the other hand, to obey a papal order which one seriously thinks is wrong would be a sin—even if one is culpably mistaken (a person may be to blame for having a false conscience, but not for acting in accordance with it). In the last analysis, conscience, however misguided, is supreme; and Newman concludes the discussion calmly, even casually, with the famous declaration:

> I add one remark. Certainly, if I am obliged to bring religion into after-dinner toasts, (which indeed does not seem quite the thing) I shall drink—to the Pope, if you please—still, to Conscience first, and to the Pope afterwards.[89]

Newman's *Lectures on the Prophetical Office* had been his first ecclesiological work and it is fitting that his last contribution to ecclesiology is the great Preface of 1877 to his new edition of the *Prophetical Office*. It also contains his final reflections on the problem of the corruption of the Church. In a letter he says that he had "long wished" to write an essay "on the conflicting interests, and therefore difficulties of the Catholic Church, because she is at once, first a devotion, secondly a philosophy, thirdly a polity." At present, as at other times, it was clear that "the philosophical instinct" had been eclipsed by the other two aspects.[90]

In the Preface Newman explains that his object is to provide an answer to one of the two important and plausible objections to the Roman Catholic Church which he had reproduced from Anglican writers in those lectures forty years ago. In the *Development of Doctrine* he had already dealt with "the contrast which modern Catholicism is said to present with the religion of the Primitive Church." Now he proposes to consider "the difference which at first sight presents itself between its formal teaching and its popular and political manifestations." It is no mere academic problem for him, as he will be "explaining, as I have long wished to do, how I myself get over difficulties which I formerly felt." And far from these difficulties decreasing since his own conversion, "It is so ordered on high that in our day Holy Church should present just that aspect to my countrymen which is most consonant with their ingrained prejudices against her."[91]

Newman's simple answer to the problem is that "such an apparent contrariety between word and deed, the abstract and the concrete, could not but take place," since the Church's "organization cannot be otherwise than complex, considering the many functions which she has to fulfil." By way of analogy, he points out how difficult it is for one and the same person to perform different roles in different public and private situations. The Church is the mystical body of Christ, who "is Prophet, Priest and, King; and after His pattern, and in human measure, Holy Church has a triple office too; not the Prophetical alone and in isolation, as [the *Lectures on the Prophetical Office*] virtually teach, but three offices, which are indivisible, though diverse, viz. teaching, rule, and sacred ministry." It follows that Christianity "is at once a philosophy, a political power, and a religious rite: as a religion, it is Holy; as a philosophy, it is Apostolic; as a political power, it is imperial, that is, One and Catholic. As a religion, its special centre of action is pastor and flock; as a philosophy, the Schools; as a rule, the Papacy and its Curia." Although the Church has always exercised the three offices,

> they were developed in their full proportions one after another, in a succession of centuries; first, in the primitive time it was recognized as a worship, springing up and spreading in the lower ranks of society. . . . Then it seized upon the intellectual and cultivated class, and created a theology and schools of learning.

Lastly it seated itself, as an ecclesiastical polity, among princes, and chose Rome for its centre.

The three different offices are based on different principles, use different means, and are liable to different corruptions:

Truth is the guiding principle of theology and theological inquiries; devotion and edification, of worship; and of government, expedience. The instrument of theology is reasoning; of worship, our emotional nature; of rule, command and coercion. Further, in man as he is, reasoning tends to rationalism; devotion to superstition and enthusiasm; and power to ambition and tyranny.

The difficulty of combining all three offices is well illustrated by the question, "What line of conduct, except on the long, the very long run, is at once edifying, expedient, and true?" Certainly, the gift of infallibility protects the Church from error not only directly in teaching but also "indirectly" in "worship and political action also"; however, "nothing but the gift of impeccability granted to her authorities would secure them from all liability to mistake in their conduct, policy, words and decisions." The problem of exercising these three very different functions "supplies the staple of those energetic charges and vivid pictures of the inconsistency, double-dealing, and deceit of the Church of Rome."[92]

Without attempting to deny the corruptions of the Church, Newman is anxious to correct his mistake in the *Prophetical Office* in blaming them on Catholic theology, by pointing out that "ambition, craft, cruelty, and superstition are not commonly the characteristic of theologians," whereas the alleged corruptions in fact "bear on their face the marks of having a popular or a political origin," and "theology, so far from encouraging them, has restrained and corrected such extravagances as have been committed, through human infirmity, in the exercise of the regal and sacerdotal powers." Indeed, he adds almost dramatically, religion is never "in greater danger than when, in consequence of national or international trou-

bles, the Schools of theology have been broken up and ceased
to be." He then gives the reason for this in some of the most
weighty words he ever wrote:

> I say, then, Theology is the fundamental and regulating principle
> of the whole Church system. It is commensurate with Revela-
> tion, and Revelation is the initial and essential idea of Christian-
> ity. It is the subject-matter, the formal cause, the expression, of
> the Prophetical Office, and, as being such, has created both the
> Regal Office and the Sacerdotal. And it has in a certain sense a
> power of jurisdiction over those offices, as being its own crea-
> tions, theologians being ever in request and in employment in
> keeping within bounds both the political and popular elements
> in the Church's constitution,—elements which are far more con-
> genial than itself to the human mind, are far more liable to
> excess and corruption. . . . [93]

Ever mindful of the need to keep a balance, Newman
promptly introduces a qualification: "Yet theology cannot always have its own way; it is too hard, too intellectual, too
exact, to be always equitable, or to be always compassion-
ate. . . ." Sometimes even a theologian in his writings has to
"let his devout nature betray itself between the joints of his
theological harness." Popular religion may, for example, reject
a more accurate translation of the Bible because to "the devotional mind what is new and strange is as repulsive, often as
dangerous, as falsehood is to the scientific. Novelty is often
error to those who are unprepared for it, from the refraction
with which it enters into their conceptions." However wrong
the condemnation of Galileo, nevertheless

> there was nothing wrong in censuring abrupt, startling, unset-
> tling, unverified disclosures . . . at once uncalled for and inop-
> portune, at a time when the limits of revealed truth had not as
> yet been ascertained. A man ought to be very sure of what he is
> saying, before he risks the chance of contradicting the word of
> God. It was safe, not dishonest, to be slow in accepting what

nevertheless turned out to be true. Here is an instance in which
the Church obliges Scripture expositors, at a given time or place,
to be tender of the popular religious sense.

People's "imaginations" have to become accustomed to religious changes, whereas "when science crosses and breaks the
received path of Revelation," religious people are criticized if
"they show hesitation to shift at a minute's warning their
position, and to accept as truths shadowy views at variance
with what they have ever been taught and have held." The
modern idea is that it is "a great moral virtue to be fearless
and thorough in inquiry into facts," whereas the "pursuit of
truth in the subject-matter of religion ... must always be
accompanied by the fear of error."[94] Elsewhere, Newman says:
"What the genius of the Church cannot bear is, changes in
thought being hurried, abrupt, violent—out of tenderness to
souls, for unlearned and narrow minded men get unsettled and
miserable. The great thing is to move all together and then
the change, as geological changes, must be very slow." In
another letter, however, he emphasizes the role of theology
in preparing the Church for changes—"it is the arena on
which questions of development and change are argued out
... it prepares the way, accustoming the mind of Catholics
to the idea of the change." Because theology also, he explains
in the same letter, "protects" dogma by "forming a large body
of doctrine which must be got through before an attack can
be made on the dogma," without theology "the dogma of the
Church would be the raw flesh without skin—nay or a tree
without leaves—for, as devotional feelings clothe the dogma
on the one hand, so does the teaching of [theology] on the
other."[95]

The distinction between theology and popular religion,
Newman argues, may be traced to the Gospel itself, and he
cites the case of the woman with the hemorrhage who hoped
to be cured by touching the cloak of Jesus, who "passed over
the superstitious act" and healed her because of her faith. In
fact, he praised her for "what might, not without reason, be

called an idolatrous act." Actually the Gospels show that the "idolatry of ignorance" is not regarded on a level with other idolatries (of wealth, for example), which, however, are not normally "shocking to educated minds." Jesus constantly insisted on the necessity of faith—"but where does He insist on the danger of superstition?"

However, the fact remains that this and other incidents in the Gospels "form an aspect of Apostolic Christianity very different from that presented" by the epistles of St. Paul. "Need men wait for the Medieval Church in order to make their complaint that the theology of Christianity does not accord with its religious manifestations?" Does "a poor Neapolitan crone, who chatters to the crucifix" do anything inherently more superstitious than the woman with the hemorrhage? Given "the ethical intelligence of the world at large," Newman remarks that he would wonder "whether that nation really had the faith, which is free in all its ranks and classes from all kinds and degrees of what is commonly considered superstition." There is no reason to be surprised if the Catholic Church, in the face of popular religion, finds it difficult "to make her Sacerdotal office keep step with her Prophetical." This applies obviously to the cult of the angels and saints, which, "though ever to be watched with jealousy by theologians, because of human infirmity and perverseness ... has a normal place in revealed Religion." For monotheism implies beings inferior to God but superior to human beings, that are able to bridge "the vast gulf which separates Him from man." And so polytheism is only "a natural sentiment corrupted." The Church's mission is not "to oppose herself to impulses" which are "both natural and legitimate," though previously "the instruments of sin, but to do her best, by a right use, to moderate and purify them." The fact that she has not always been successful simply shows that "there will ever be a marked contrariety between the professions of her theology and the ways and doings of a Catholic country."

Moreover, the Church allows much more freedom in devotion, which is "of a subjective and personal nature," than in

doctrine. This contrast is accentuated if "ecclesiastical authority takes part with popular sentiment against a theological
decision." A very early example would be the occasion at
Antioch when St. Peter stopped associating with converts
from paganism because of pressure from converts from Juda-
ism, a lapse for which he was rebuked by St. Paul. However,
Paul himself was ready to conform to Jewish customs when
necessary, and the principle of "accommodation"—though it
may be misapplied, as perhaps in the case of the Jesuit mis-
sionaries' adoption of Chinese customs—has always been
practiced by Christians since the earliest time.[96]

The theological office of the Church, then, may find itself
in opposition to both the so-called political and pastoral offices. But equally, the political office may come into conflict
with the other two offices. This office is, in fact, essential if
the Church is to preserve her independence and freedom of
action—as is illustrated by the Orthodox Church, "which has
lost its political life, while its doctrine, and its ritual and
devotional system, have little that can be excepted against."
Like "a sovereign State," the Church has "to consolidate her
several portions, to enlarge her territory, to keep up and to
increase her various populations in this ever-dying, ever-nas-
cent world, in which to be stationary is to lose ground, and
to repose is to fail." So important is this aspect of the Church
that a point of theology may at times actually be "determined
on its expediency relatively to the Church's Catholicity," that
is, "by the logic of facts, which at times overrides all positive
laws and prerogatives, and reaches in its effective force to the
very frontiers of immutable truths."[97] The interests of the
Church may override apparently decisive theological arguments, as when Pope St. Stephen decided that heretical bap-
tisms were after all valid (a view later accepted by theologians).

The essay concludes with the reflection that "whatever is
great refuses to be reduced to human rule, and to be made
consistent in its many aspects with itself." There should be
no cause for surprise, then, if the Church "is an instance of

the same law, presenting to us an admirable consistency and unity in word and deed, as her general characteristic, but crossed and discredited now and then by apparent anomalies."[98] These exceptions may prove the rule, but it is important to stress once again that Newman is only concerned with a general rule: he is not writing the kind of systematic theology which would provide a blueprint for the Church's constitution. Indeed, it is precisely because the Church is a living body that it is not possible to draw an exact diagram of her internal workings. And it is especially difficult to describe at all schematically that conflict which is for Newman an integral part of the Church's life, the creative tension between her three offices. As in the last chapter of the *Apologia*, guidelines and general principles are offered, but always on the understanding that the necessary demarcations and limitations are drawn pragmatically rather than theoretically, realistically rather than ideally. There had been a change since those early days when the problem was whether the theory of the "Via Media" actually fitted the existing Church it was supposed to delineate. There was no difficulty now about the reality of the Church: the question rather was to find a "view" (to use Newman's favorite word) which would account for the apparently discordant, even apparently incompatible, features of a very complex, because living, Church.

It would be wrong to complete this brief study of Newman's achievement as a theologian without recognizing that his theological contribution is much larger than any account of his specifically theological works can suggest. Far less a professional theologian than a Christian thinker, practically everything he wrote is of theological significance. It is not surprising that his unsystematic, richly varied work has often suggested that he belongs more to the world of patristic than to that of modern theology. "St. Bernard is called the last of the Fathers because in him dogma and piety and literature are still one. . . . Newman, who leaves later developments on one side, took over where St. Bernard left off, and perhaps should be allowed to succeed to his title."[99]

5

THE WRITER

APART FROM A VERSE ROMANCE which he and a friend published as undergraduates, Newman's first publication was an article he contributed to an encyclopedia in 1824. It was a lengthy essay on Cicero, whom he called "the greatest master of composition that the world has seen."[1] Years later he was to acknowledge Cicero's important influence on his own writing: "As to patterns for imitation, the only master of style I have ever had (which is strange considering the differences of the languages) is Cicero. I think I owe a great deal to him, and as far as I know to no one else."[2] But Cicero seems not only to have influenced his prose style. According to his brother, Francis, Newman learned his skill as a controversialist from the Roman orator.[3] Certainly, in the article Newman pays tribute to the rhetorical art of Cicero: "He accounts for everything so naturally, makes trivial circumstances tell so happily, so adroitly converts apparent objections into confirmations of his argument, connects independent facts with such ease and plausibility, that it becomes impossible to entertain a question on the truth of his statement." He also recognizes the satirist in Cicero when he draws attention to his powers of "raillery" and "irony."[4]

Newman has been called "a controversialist of superb gifts, perhaps the most remarkable in the history of English letters."[5] The judgment indicates the nature of his literary achievement: for the two indispensable gifts of the controversialist are those of rhetoric and satire. Newman's claims as a writer have been too often underestimated by literary critics and historians for whom his achievement consists principally of his autobiography, the *Apologia*, and to a much lesser extent his two novels and poetry, which are recognized to be of interest, and even of some originality, but hardly of any major significance. As for the *Apologia*, the four chapters which tell the story of Newman's religious development are unique in his published *oeuvre*, if only because they so deliberately eschew both controversy and rhetoric and satire; but on the other hand they are to a considerable extent the record of past controversies, and abundantly documented with copious quotations from controversial writings. The last chapter and the preface and notes containing material from the original controversy with Charles Kingsley belong, however, to the mainstream of Newman's writings.

I

So many of Newman's works are controversial writings, evincing both rhetorical and satirical art. But even apart from his brilliance as a rhetorician and satirist, Newman is a consummate controversialist in a perfectly direct and straightforward way. One thinks, for example, of the famous power of rejoinder in his letters, which, in the duel with Kingsley, he practically raised to a new literary form.

The literature of controversy owes a debt to Dr. Thomas Arnold of Rugby, for it was he who elicited from Newman at the beginning of the Tractarian Movement the first of many splendid snubs. To the report that Arnold was upset because he had heard that Newman had questioned whether he was really a Christian, Newman responded that while he could not remember saying the words attributed to him, it was true that "as far as" he understood Arnold's "ecclesiastical principles," he judged them to be "unscriptural, unchristian, and open to ecclesiastical censure"—but at the same time he was happy to assure the latitudinarian headmaster of Rugby that even where "the essential Christian character" was lacking, "there may yet be piety of an irregular and uncertain kind, which of course has its praise."[6] In the course of his career, Newman was to pen many more snubs, which, whatever their moral justification, have, from a literary point of view, a classic quality of their own. The most famous of these snubs is the one administered to the egregious Roman courtier, Monsignor Talbot:

> I have received your letter, inviting me to preach next Lent in your Church at Rome, to "an audience of Protestants more educated than could ever be the case in England."
> However, Birmingham people have souls; and I have neither taste nor talent for the sort of work, which you cut out for me: and I beg to decline your offer[.][7]

But the solemn, stately snub which Newman sent to his former patron, Cardinal Wiseman, when pressed to visit the dying Father Faber, who Newman knew had intrigued behind his back with the Cardinal, is perhaps even more perfect.

> I thank your Eminence for the feeling which dictated your Eminence's letter.
> I am perfectly aware of the hopeless state in which Fr Faber lies.
> Your Eminence will be glad to know that Fr Faber has already been informed by me, not only of my wish to see him, but of the precise time when I hope to have that sad satisfaction[.][8]

Ripostes of a robust kind came as naturally as snubs to the great controversialist. Of one attack on him that appeared in a newspaper at the height of the Oxford Movement, he wrote:

> There is a great fat lie, a lie to the back bone, and in all its component parts, and in its soul and body, inside and out, in all sides of it, and in its very origin, in the Record. . . . It has no element of truth in it—it is born of a lie—its father and mother are lies and all its ancestry—and to complete it, it is about me.[9]

The gloating fascination with which Newman pursues the metaphor is characteristic of the kind of gleefully grotesque imagery he would develop later in his satirical writings. The extraordinary rumors that spread in the early 1860's (before the *Apologia*) that Newman had left or was about to leave the Roman Catholic Church also provoked some superb rejoinders. Of one extreme Protestant correspondent who had announced in a provincial newspaper that the celebrated "clerical pervert" was now a skeptic living in Paris, Newman wrote to the editor:

> In an age of light, where in the world has the unfortunate man been living? Of what select circle is he the oracle? What bad luck has seduced him into print? What has ailed him to take up a position so false, that the Law might come down upon him, and every Englishman must cry shame upon him?[10]

But the letter that attracted the most notoriety was the one Newman sent to a London newspaper, in which he attempted once and for all to squash the rumors:

> Therefore, in order to give them full satisfaction, if I can, I do hereby profess *ex animo*, with an absolute internal assent and consent, that Protestantism is the dreariest of possible religions; that the thought of the Anglican service makes me shiver, and the thought of the Thirty-nine Articles makes me shudder. Return to the Church of England! no; "the net is broken, and we are delivered." I should be a consummate fool (to use a mild term) if in my old age I left "the land flowing with milk and honey" for the city of confusion and the house of bondage.[11]

Newman's great hour, of course, as a controversialist came with the Kingsley controversy. In perhaps the most vibrantly indignant passage he ever wrote, the appeal to analogy, which is such a marked feature of both his thought and rhetoric, as well as of his polemic and satire, is put to brilliant effect:

> I, on my side, have long thought, even before I was a Catholic, that the Protestant system, as such, leads to a lax observance of

the rule of purity; Protestants think that the Catholic system, as
such, leads to a lax observance of the rule of truth. I am very
sorry that they should think so, but I cannot help it; I lament
their mistake, but I bear it as I may. If Mr. Kingsley had said no
more than this, I should not have felt it necessary to criticize
such an ordinary remark. But, as I should be committing a crime,
heaping dirt upon my soul, and storing up for myself remorse and
confusion of face at a future day, if I applied my abstract belief
of the latent sensuality of Protestantism, on *a priori* reasoning,
to individuals, to living persons, to authors and men of name,
and said (not to make disrespectful allusion to the living) that
Bishop Van Mildert, or the Rev. Dr. Spry, or Dean Milner, or
the Rev. Charles Simeon "informs us that chastity for its own
sake need not be, and on the whole ought not to be, a virtue
with the Anglican clergy," and then, when challenged for the
proof, said, "*Vide* Van Mildert's Bampton Lectures and Simeon's
Skeleton Sermons *passim*;" and, as I should only make the matter
still worse, if I pointed to flagrant instances of paradoxical divines or of bad clergymen among Protestants . . . so, in like
manner, for a writer, when he is criticizing definite historical
facts of the sixteenth century, which stand or fall on their own
merits, to go out of his way to have a fling at an unpopular name,
living but "down," and boldly to say . . . of *me*, "Father Newman
informs us that Truth for its own sake *need not be, and on the whole
ought not to be,* a virtue with the Roman clergy," and to be thus
brilliant and antithetical (save the mark!) in the very cause of
Truth, is a proceeding of so special a character as to lead me to
exclaim, after the pattern of the celebrated saying, "O Truth,
how many lies are told in thy name!"[12]

The sustained protest begins with a series of five tersely abrupt
sentences that culminate in one single long sentence which
actually constitutes over three-quarters of the whole passage
and which rises to a veritable crescendo of indignation, not
articulated in formal prose but expressed in the stressed accent
and rhythm of conversational idiom.

The disingenuous "apology" that Kingsley offered to publish

had the merit of provoking Newman into writing a marvelously comic dialogue where again he uses the ordinary speaking voice to great dramatic effect.

Mr. Kingsley begins then by exclaiming,—"O the chicanery, the
wholesale fraud, the vile hypocrisy, the conscience-killing tyranny of Rome! We have not far to seek for an evidence of it.
There's Father Newman to wit: one living specimen is worth a
hundred dead ones. He, a Priest writing of Priests, tells us that
lying is never any harm."

I interpose: "You are taking a most extraordinary liberty with
my name. If I have said this, tell me when and where."

Mr. Kingsley replies: "You said it, Reverend Sir, in a Sermon
which you preached, when a Protestant, as Vicar of St. Mary's,
and published in 1844; and I could read you a very salutary
lecture on the effects which that Sermon had at the time on my
own opinion of you."

I make answer: "Oh . . . Not, it seems, as a Priest speaking of
Priests;—but let us have the passage."

Mr. Kingsley relaxes: "Do you know, I like your tone. From
your tone I rejoice, greatly rejoice, to be able to believe that you
did not mean what you said."

I rejoin: "Mean it! I maintain I never said it, whether as a
Protestant or as a Catholic."

Mr. Kingsley replies: "I waive that point."

I object: "Is it possible! What? waive the main question! I
either said it or I didn't. You have made a monstrous charge
against me; direct, distinct, public. You are bound to prove it as
directly, as distinctly, as publicly;—or to own you can't."

"Well," says Mr. Kingsley, "if you are quite sure you did not
say it, I'll take your word for it; I really will."

My word! I am dumb. Somehow I thought that it was my word
that happened to be on trial. The word of a Professor of lying,
that he does not lie!

But Mr. Kingsley re-assures me: "We are both gentlemen,"
he says: "I have done as much as one English gentleman can
expect from another."

I begin to see: he thought me a gentleman at the very time that he said I taught lying on system. After all, it is not I, but it is Mr. Kingsley who did not mean what he said."[13]

Much of the polemical material that introduced the first edition (1864) of the *Apologia* was dropped in the second edition (1865) in favor of a brief preface, which, however, was enlarged in the final edition (1873) with extracts from the material that had been omitted. Certainly the original two polemical pamphlets contain some superb invective which may grate on modern religious ears but which ought to appeal to anyone with an ear for the English language and a taste for the literature of controversy.

He need not commit himself to a definite accusation against me, such as requires definite proof and admits of definite refutation; for he has two strings to his bow;—when he is thrown off his balance on the one leg, he can recover himself by the use of the other. If I demonstrate that I am not a knave, he may exclaim, "Oh, but you are a fool!" and when I demonstrate that I am not a fool, he may turn round and retort, "Well, then, you are a knave. . . ."

I am sitting at home without a thought of Mr. Kingsley; he wantonly breaks in upon me. . . . " . . . If you have not broken one commandment, let us see whether we cannot convict you of the breach of another. If you are not a swindler or forger, you are guilty of arson or burglary. . . . What does it matter to you who are going off the stage, to receive a slight additional daub upon a character so deeply stained already?"[14]

And inevitably, the polemic merges into satire:

It is good luck for me that the scene of my labours was not at Moscow or Damascus. . . . Then you might ascribe to me a more deadly craft than mere quibbling and lying; in Spain I should have been an Inquisitor, with my rack in the background; I should have had a concealed dagger in Sicily; at Venice I should have brewed poison; in Turkey I should have been the Sheik-el-Islam with my bowstring. . . .[15]

II

Newman's first real attempts at satire appear in a couple of letters he wrote in 1833 while on his Mediterranean tour. Once again they were stimulated, or rather provoked, by Dr. Arnold and the news of his new book arguing for religious comprehensiveness as the only way of avoiding the disestablishment of the Church of England. In the first Newman says of Arnold's "very comprehensive" plan:

> If I understand it right, all sects (the Church inclusive) are to hold their meetings in the Parish Church—though not at the same hour of course. He excludes Quakers and Roman Catholics—yet even with this exclusion surely there will be too many sects in some places for one day? ... If I might propose an amendment, I should say, pass an Act to oblige some persuasions to *change* the Sunday—if you have two Sundays in a week, it is plain you could easily accommodate any probable number of sects. ... Nor would this interfere with the Jews' worship (which of course is to be in the Church)—they are too few to take up a whole day. Luckily the Mohammedan holiday is already on a Friday; so there will be no difficulty of arrangement in that quarter.[16]

The mock solemnity of this passage is followed by a more openly sarcastic response to the Arnold proposal, encouraging a more liberal comprehensiveness:

> he is said to exclude the Jews, Roman Catholics, and Quakers from the Churches—this seems to me illiberal. The only objection I can fancy is the want of time in one day for these in addition to those already admitted to participation in the Churches—I am aware the Quakers remain an indefinite period at one sitting—and it would not do to keep the Sandemonians or the Socinians waiting—there must be a punctuality, if all are to be accommodated. Yet I think the difficulty might be met by forcing the Evangelicals to keep their Sunday on the Saturday. ... The Jews could take Saturday too—and the Roman Catho-

lics would come in for Sunday in place of the Evangelicals. The
Mahometan Feast being Friday would not interfere. —Or on the
whole, since it is immaterial on what day the Christian festival
is kept, the whole week might be divided among the various
denomination of Christians. —I have another plan, which I hold
to be altogether original and is the firstfruits of my late conversion and runs Dr A hard. It is to allot the 24 Colleges and Halls
of Oxford among the various denominations—in this way you
might meet the difficulty about subscription. . . . I would allow
of exchanges or conversions. . . .[17]

Newman, of course, had very strong theological objections
to Arnold's latitudinarianism, but what he satirizes so effectively, by drawing out the logic of Arnold's comprehensive
plan to its absurd conclusion, is the unreality of ignoring real
religious differences.

Naturally, it would be an exaggeration to suggest that all
Newman's satire is directed at the absurdity of the "unreal."
His satirical humor is not confined to this, either at this period
or later. In his "Letters on the Church of the Fathers," for
example, which he also wrote in 1833, he remarks that "St.
Ambrose and his brethren" might "have as reasonably disbe-
lieved the possible existence of parsonages and pony carriages
in the nineteenth century, as we the existence of martyrs and
miracles in the primitive age."[18] Amused by the fury of the
Evangelicals at the success of Tractarianism, he wrote (in a
private letter), "They put me in mind of a naughty child put
atop of the bookcase, very frightened, but very furious."[19]
Confidence in the Tractarian cause brought forth many a
gleeful sarcasm at the expense of the worldly established
Church:

> Doubtless, in the long run, the gridiron of St. Laurence would
> be found a more effectual guarantee of Church property than a
> coronation oath or an act of parliament. A broiling here and
> there, once or twice a century, would, on the whole, have en-
> sured to the Church the unmolested enjoyment of her property
> throughout her dominions down to this day.[20]

The paradoxical irony, which Newman enjoys bringing out, is that it is precisely establishment which has enslaved the Church:

> She has been among strangers; statesmen, lawyers, and soldiers frisked and prowled around: creatures wild or tame have held a parliament over her, but still she has wanted some one to converse with, to repose on, to consult, to love. The State indeed . . . has thought it unreasonable in her, that she could not find in a lion and a unicorn a sufficient object for her affections. It has set her to keep order in the land, to restrain enthusiasm, and to rival and so discountenance "Popery." . . .[21]

It remains true, however, that just as the theme of the "real" and the "unreal" is a, or even *the*, distinguishing feature of Newman's thought, so, not surprisingly, it does to a very large degree inform the vision of the satirist. Time and again, it is the inherent unreality of an opposing religious or theological point of view that Newman satirizes. While still an Anglican, he came to be struck by the contradictions involved in literally believing that the pope was the "Antichrist": but what really aroused his powers of sarcasm was the thought of the "private life" of the chief source of this tradition for English Protestants, a divine called Thomas Newton, to whom we owe perhaps the funniest lines Newman ever wrote:

> . . . a man so idolatrous of comfort, so liquorish of preferment, whose most fervent aspiration apparently was that he might ride in a carriage and sleep on down, whose keenest sorrow that he could not get a second appointment without relinquishing the first, who cast a regretful look back upon his dinner while he was at supper, and anticipated his morning chocolate in his evening muffins, who will say that this is the man, not merely to unchurch, but to smite, to ban, to wither the whole of Christendom for many centuries, and the greater part of it even in his own day. . . .

The marvelous inconsistency in such a man attempting to "establish the paradox" that St. Charles Borromeo "sucked the breast of Babylon, and that Pascal died in her arms" is as ridiculous as it is unreal.[22] Elsewhere Newman enjoys satirizing even more glaring contradictions in Protestantism:

> "We [Protestants] uphold the pure unmutilated Scripture; the Bible, and the Bible only, is the religion of Protestants; the Bible and our own sense of the Bible. We claim a sort of parliamentary privilege to interpret laws in our own way, and not to suffer an appeal to any court beyond ourselves. We know, and we view it with consternation, that all antiquity runs counter to our interpretation; and therefore, alas, the Church was corrupt from *very* early times indeed. But mind, we hold all this in a truly Catholic spirit, not in bigotry. We allow in others the right of private judgment, and confess that we, as others, are fallible men. We confess facts are against us; we do but claim the liberty of theorizing in spite of them. Far be it from us to say that we are certainly right; we only say that the whole early Church was certainly wrong. We do not impose our own belief on any one; we only say that those who take the contrary side are Papists, firebrands, persecutors, madmen, zealots, bigots, and an insult to the nineteenth century."[23]

Here the insistent rhythm of indignation which Newman used so effectively in his controversy with Charles Kingsley is turned to purely satiric effect against the speaker(s).

The Protestant tenet which in Newman's view opened the floodgates to religious liberalism is also satirized in one of the most exuberant satirical passages of the Anglican period. And we notice again that what fuels the satire is the inherent inconsistency of the Protestant principle of "private judgment":

> Is it not sheer wantonness and cruelty in Baptist, Independent, Irvingite, Wesleyan, Establishment-man, Jumper, and Mormonite, to delight in trampling on and crushing these manifestations of their own pure and precious charter, instead of dutifully and reverently exalting, at Bethel, or at Dan, each instance of it, as it occurs, to the gaze of its professing votaries? If a staunch

Protestant's daughter turns Roman, and betakes herself to a convent, why does he not exult in the occurrence? Why does he not
give a public breakfast, or hold a meeting, or erect a memorial,
or write a pamphlet in honour of her, and of the great undying
principle she has so gloriously vindicated? Why is he in this base,
disloyal style muttering about priests, and Jesuits, and the horrors
of nunneries, in solution of the phenomenon, when he has the
fair and ample form of Private Judgment rising before his eyes,
and pleading with him. . . . All this would lead us to suspect that
the doctrine of private judgment, in its simplicity, purity, and
integrity,—private judgment, all private judgment, and nothing
but private judgment,—is held by very few persons indeed; and
that the great mass of the population are either stark unbelievers
in it, or deplorably dark about it; and that even the minority
who are in a manner faithful to it, have glossed and corrupted
the true sense of it by a miserably faulty reading, and hold, not
the right of private judgment, but the private right of judgment;
in other words, their own private right, and no one else's. . . .[24]

It is a pity that such superb satire is apparently unknown to
the literary guides and histories which prefer to speak of the
charm and sincerity of the *Apologia* and the eloquence of the
Discourses on university education, practically ignoring the
less smooth and sharper side of Newman. Since the Victorian
critic R. H. Hutton first drew attention to Newman's powers
of irony and sarcasm, almost no further attention has been
paid by literary critics to this striking aspect of his art.

The only sustained satirical writing that Newman produced
as an Anglican were the letters which comprise the *Tamworth
Reading Room* (1841), which contains some of the most brilliant prose he ever wrote.[25] In it he attacks the modern belief
in the power of knowledge to replace religion as the bond of
morality and society. How, for instance, can science produce
moral effects? "Can the process be analyzed and drawn out,
or does it act like a dose or charm which comes into general
use empirically?" It would appear that "To know is one thing,
to do is another"—an objection, of course, which the Utilitar-

ian philosopher Jeremy Bentham would answer by saying "that the knowledge which carries virtue along with it, is the knowledge how to take care of number one," for "Useful Knowledge is that which tends to make us more useful to ourselves;—a most definite and intelligible account of the matter, and needing no explanation." But what do Sir Robert Peel and Lord Brougham, the two political exponents of the heresy Newman is assailing, suppose is the connection between knowledge and morals?

> When a husband is gloomy, or an old woman peevish and fretful, those who are about them do all they can to keep dangerous topics and causes of offence out of the way, and think themselves lucky, if, by such skilful management, they get through the day without an outbreak. When a child cries, the nurserymaid dances it about, or points to the pretty black horses out of window, or shows how ashamed poll-parrot or poor puss must be of its tantrums. Such is the sort of prescription which Sir Robert Peel offers to the good people of Tamworth. He makes no pretence of subduing the giant nature, in which we were born, of smiting the loins of the domestic enemies of our peace, of overthrowing passion and fortifying reason; he does but offer to bribe the foe for the nonce with gifts which will avail for that purpose just so long as they *will* avail, and no longer.

Lord Brougham similarly

> offers us a philosophy of expedients: he shows us how to live by medicine. Digestive pills half an hour before dinner, and a posset at bedtime at the best; and at the worst, dram-drinking and opium,—the very remedy against broken hearts, or remorse of conscience, which is in request among the many, in gin-palaces *not* intellectual.

But "who was ever consoled in real trouble by the small beer of literature or science?" Or when, Newman asks, "was a choleric temperament ever brought under by a scientific King Canute planting his professor's chair before the rising waves?" Anyway, it is not very realistic to imagine that the "pleasures" of "intellectual pursuit and conquest" will not be "outbid in the market by gratifications much closer at hand, and on a level with the meanest capacity." The colloquial tone of voice only adds to the sense of the outrageously incongruous: "Such is this new art of living, offered to the labouring classes,—we will say, for instance, in a severe winter, snow on the ground, glass falling, bread rising, coal at 20d. the cwt., and no work." The most sarcastic of satirists never managed to write anything better than this:

> that the mind is changed by a discovery, or saved by a diversion, and can thus be amused into immortality,—that grief, anger, cowardice, self-conceit, pride, or passion, can be subdued by an examination of shells or grasses, or inhaling of gases, or chipping of rocks, or calculating the longitude, is the veriest of pretences which sophist or mountebank ever professed to a gaping auditory. If virtue be a mastery over the mind, if its end be action, if its perfection be inward order, harmony, and peace, we must seek it in graver and holier places than in Libraries and Reading-rooms.[26]

As a great proponent of realism himself, Newman has a certain reluctant respect for that "stern realist" Bentham (whose "system has nothing ideal about it"), even though "he limits his realism to things which he can see, hear, taste, touch, and handle." But nothing could be more unreal than to imagine that knowledge ever "healed a wounded heart" or "changed a sinful one." The imagery used is disconcertingly tactile, culminating in an image of physical confinement to satirize the theorizing of Brougham and Peel (the figure of imprisonment would be put to similar effect in the later satirical writings):

> Christianity raises men from earth, for it comes from heaven; but human morality creeps, struts, or frets upon the earth's level, without wings to rise. The Knowledge School does not contemplate raising man above himself; it merely aims at disposing of his existing powers and tastes, as is most convenient, or is practi-

cable under circumstances. It finds him, like the victims of the French Tyrant, doubled up in a cage in which he can neither lie, stand, sit, nor kneel, and its highest desire is to find an attitude in which his unrest may be least.[27]

Lord Brougham, who "understands that something more is necessary for man's happiness than self-love" and that "man has affections and aspirations which Bentham does not take account of," dismisses Christianity as "dogmatism": "Human nature wants recasting, but Lord Brougham is all for tinkering it."[28] Sir Robert Peel, on the other hand, is sure that the study of science will lead to religious faith. But, Newman warns ironically, "The way is long, and there are not a few half-way houses and traveller's rests along it. . . . " Anyway, "common sense and practical experience" show that if people "give their leisure and curiosity to this world, they will have none left for the next." He wonders, incidentally, why the Tamworth Reading-room only admits "*virtuous* women" as members—

A very emphatic silence is maintained about women not virtuous. What does this mean? Does it mean to exclude them, while bad *men* are admitted? Is this accident, or design, sinister and insidious, against a portion of the community? What has virtue to do with a Reading-room? It is to *make* its members virtuous. . . .

How inconsistent that "bigotry should have left the mark of its hoof" on so liberal a philosophy![29]

The first book Newman published as a Catholic was a novel, *Loss and Gain: The Story of a Convert* (1848). One very noticeable similarity between the hero, an Oxford undergraduate called Charles Reding, and the author is the same preoccupation with the *real* and the *unreal*. The theme of reality versus unreality, which runs through the book, is the source of some very effective and funny satire. One character, Mr. Vincent, a tutor, "who was for ever mistaking shams for truths," and to avoid extremes prides himself on "holding all opinions," however contradictory, provides a marvelous comic eulogy of the comprehensiveness of the Church of England:

"Our Church," he said, "admitted of great liberty of thought within her pale. Even our greatest divines differed from each other in many respects; nay, Bishop Taylor differed from himself. It was a great principle in the English Church. Her true children agree to differ. In truth, there is that robust, masculine, noble independence in the English mind, which refuses to be tied down to artificial shapes, but is like, I will say, some great and beautiful production of nature—a tree, which is rich in foliage and fantastic in limb, no sickly denizen of the hothouse, or helpless dependent of the garden wall, but in careless magnificence sheds its fruits upon the free earth, for the bird of the air and the beast of the field, and all sorts of cattle, to eat thereof and rejoice."[30]

The intended contrast between two representatives of a real and an unreal religion is caricatured in a comic scene when Charles, by now close to reception into the Roman Catholic Church, comes across in a religious bookshop at Bath another Anglo-Catholic friend from Oxford, White, who had once idealized clerical celibacy, but is now a clergyman engaged to be married. Again, it is the unreality rather than the comfortable worldliness of the Anglican clergy which disgusts Charles and his author. White's bride cannot remember the name of a book she wanted. Can it be "The Catholic Parsonage?" or "Modified Celibacy?" No, it is "Abbeys and Abbots"—"'I want to get some hints for improving the rectory windows when we get home; and our church wants, you know, a porch for the poor people.'"[31]

In the advertisement to the novel, Newman had been careful to deny that any of the characters was properly representative of Tractarianism, and in a later letter he stressed that his satire was directed against the same "unreality and inconsistency" which he had laughed at as an Anglican, in other words at the "*abuse*" of Tractarian views.[32] Thus there can be no question about the seriousness of Tractarian insistence on fasting, or its preoccupation with the Church's calendar—in spite of Mr. Vincent's order to the astonished college servant to check if it was a fasting day: "'The Vigil of St. Peter, you mean, Watkins; I thought so. Then let us have a plain beef-steak and a saddle of mutton; no Portugal onions, Watkins, or currant-jelly; and some simple pudding, Charlotte pudding, Watkins—that will do.'"[33]

The "honeymoon" years of Newman's Catholic life after his conversion saw the flowering of his satirical genius. Satire even comes quite prominently into his sermons of this period. In one he remarks: "The world professes to supply all that we need, as if we were sent into it for the sake of being sent here, and for nothing beyond the sending," so that "It is a great favour to have an introduction to this august world." In another he comments on so-called Bible Christians, "I can fancy a man magisterially expounding St. Paul's Epistle to the Galatians or to the Ephesians, who would be better content with the writer's absence than his sudden re-appearance among us. . . . "[34] For English Protestants, who "shrink from the great road of travel which God has appointed" and "run . . . their own private conveyance . . . on their own track," there is no "calumny too gross" and "no imputation on us so monstrous which they will not drink up greedily like water," and because there is "a demand for such fabrications," there is "a consequent supply" of slanders against Catholics, who are "fair game for all comers," and who can only expect "to be treated as shadows of the past, names a thousand miles away, abstractions, commonplaces, historical figures, or dramatic properties, waste ground on which any load of abuse may be shot, the convenient conductors of a distempered political atmosphere."[35] The Englishman's boast, his "private judgment," is in fact little more than the "passive impression" which he receives from his "intellectual servants," the periodicals and newspapers that are employed to tell him "what to think and what to say," the only condition being that this "cheap knowledge" should be "ready to hand, as he has his table-cloth laid for his breakfast." Accordingly, in religious matters the Englishman "is bent on action, but as to opinion he takes what comes, only he bargains not to be teased or troubled about it," with the result that he "is satisfied to walk about, dressed as he is" and very much "resents the idea of interference," for "it is an insult to be told that God has spoken and superseded investigation," particularly as "he thinks the Englishman knows more about God's dealings with men, than any one else."[36] Just as Dickens caricatured the social pretensions of the great Victorian middle class and Matthew Arnold sneered at its cultural superficiality, so Newman satirized its religious parochialism and shallowness.

But it was in the two series of lectures which he gave in 1850 and 1851 that Newman for the first time gave full expression to his powers of satire. In *Lectures on Certain Difficulties felt by Anglicans in submitting to the Catholic Church* (1850), Newman turns his satirical wit against Anglo-Catholicism, and precisely against that very aspect of it of which he himself had been so uneasily conscious even as he was attempting to construct a positive theology of the "Via Media"—namely, its *unreality*. For the fact of the matter is, Newman argues, that Anglo-Catholics do not really belong to the Church of England at all. They look up to their "Mother" church and find her "silent, ambiguous, unsympathetic, sullen, and even hostile," "with ritual mutilated, sacraments defective, precedents inconsistent, articles equivocal, canons obsolete, courts Protestant, and synods suspended; scouted by the laity, scorned by men of the world, hated and blackened."[37] The Catholic Church, which "is the one ark of salvation," is waiting to receive Anglo-Catholics "who have thrown themselves" from the "wreck" of the Established Church upon "the waves, or are clinging to its rigging, or are sitting in heaviness and despair upon its side."[38] The "power of a nation's will" becomes the "giant ocean" which "has suddenly swelled and heaved, and majestically yet masterfully snaps the cables of the smaller craft which lie upon its bosom, and strands them upon the beach," so that the great high Anglican divines, "names mighty in their generation, are broken and wrecked."[39] Anglo-Catholic theology itself is "most uncon-

genial and heterogeneous, floating upon it, a foreign substance, like oil upon the water."[40] Anglo-Catholic theologians
had appealed to the authority of the Fathers:

> there they found a haven of rest; thence they looked out upon
> the troubled surge of human opinion and upon the crazy vessels
> which were labouring, without chart or compass, upon it. Judge
> then of their dismay, when, according to the Arabian tale, on
> their striking their anchors into the supposed soil, lighting their
> fires on it, and fixing in it the poles of their tents, suddenly their
> island began to move, to heave, to splash, to frisk to and fro, to
> dive, and at last to swim away, spouting out inhospitable jets of
> water upon the credulous mariners who had made it their
> home.[41]

What had been presented as a profound shock of tragic dimen-
sions can now be depicted in comic imagery, which is also
deployed against other targets.

Unlike their high Anglican counterparts, the Evangelical
clergy "glide forward rapidly and proudly down the stream" of
the age which is so congenial to them.[42] Whereas the spiritual
power of the Catholic Church is real though imperceptible—
in the same way that the air which "gives way, and . . . returns
again . . . exerts a gentle but constant pressure on every
side"[43]—the faith of Protestants is "a sickly child," brought
out "of doors only on fine days"; and Protestants lose their
"vision of the Unseen" "if they turn about their head, or
change their posture ever so little," so "they keep the exhibition of their faith for high days and great occasions, when it
comes forth with sufficient pomp and gravity of language, and
ceremonial of manner."[44] The Established Church is pictured
as a "huge creature" which, in spite of the Tractarian Movement, "has steadily gone on its own way, eating, drinking,
sleeping, and working, fulfilling its nature," and which,
oblivious of the defections to Rome, "showed no consciousness of its loss, but shook itself, and went about its work as of
old time."[45]

The marvelous comic imagery is meant to laugh Anglo-Catholics out of their unreal fantasies and pretensions. They had invested their bishops with unfamiliar apostolic powers, and these same bishops had then

> fearlessly handselled their Apostolic weapons upon the Apostolical party. . . . It was a solemn war-dance, which they executed round victims, who by their very principles were bound hand and foot, and could only eye with disgust and perplexity this most unaccountable movement, on the part of their "holy Fathers, the representatives of the Apostles, and the Angels of the Churches."[46]

The very first of the *Tracts for the Times* wished

> nothing better for the Bishops of the Establishment than martyrdom. . . . It was easy to foresee what response the Establishment would make to its officious defenders, as soon as it could recover from its surprise; but experience was necessary to teach this to men who knew more of St. Athanasius than of the Privy Council or the Court of Arches.[47]

In place of a teaching authority, the Anglo-Catholic theologian has to put forward his "own private researches into St. Chrysostom and St. Augustine," which his followers are required to accept unreservedly as "the teaching of the old Fathers, and of your Mother the Church of England."[48] Newman employs imagery uncannily reminiscent of the grotesque imprisoning imagery of Dickens, to express the discomfort of the Anglo-Catholic's life in the Church of England, where

> there is no lying, or standing, or sitting, or kneeling, or stooping there, in any possible attitude . . . when you would rest your head, your legs are forced out between the Articles, and when you would relieve your back, your head strikes against the Prayer Book; when, place yourselves as you will, on the right side or the left and try to keep as still as you can, your flesh is ever being punctured and probed by the stings of Bishops, laity, and nine-tenths of the Clergy buzzing about you. . . .[49]

A totally unoriginal image can be used to devastating effect, as when with the gentlest irony Newman recommends the Anglo-Catholic to

> have nothing to do with a "Branch Church." You have had enough experience of branch churches already, and you know very well what they are. Depend upon it, such as is one, such is another. They may differ in accidents certainly; but, after all, a branch is a branch, and no branch is a tree. Depend upon it, my brethren, it is not worth while leaving one branch for another.[50]

In national churches, doctrine is not determined by Bible or tradition "but by its tendency to minister to the peace and repose of the community, to the convenience and comfort of Downing Street, Lambeth, and Exeter Hall."[51] A national church reflects the will of the nation, which reflects the will of the world: "Provided it could gain one little islet in the ocean, one foot upon the coast, if it could cheapen tea by sixpence a pound, or make its flag respected among the Esquimaux or Otaheitans, at the cost of a hundred lives and a hundred souls, it would think it a very good bargain."[52]

Newman always considered his next book, *Lectures on the Present Position of Catholics in England* (1851), to be his "best written book."[53] It is certainly his best satirical work and as such deserves a high place in the history of English satire. The fact that it is hardly known or read—even by Newman scholars—is no doubt easily explained: because the subject is so explicitly religious, not to say Catholic,—and the title does not help—literary critics and historians are unlikely to read it, while its highly polemical style is hardly calculated to appeal to an age which is easily embarrassed by the robustness of Victorian religious controversy.[54] And yet in its day it was admired by a writer like George Eliot.

The target of Newman's satire now is not the unreality of Anglo-Catholicism, but the unreal nature of the virulent anti-Catholicism of Protestant England. He begins the first lecture by announcing that his intention is to investigate the reasons for the universal prejudice against Catholics ("how it is we are cried out against by the very stones, and bricks, and tiles, and chimney-pots"), a prejudice which "is not only a trial to flesh and blood, but a discomfort to the reason and imagination."[55] His aim is to show that the actual prejudice is founded not on reason but on illusory imagination. Scandalous stories circulated against Catholics may be proved to have no basis in fact, and yet an "impression" has been "created or deepened . . . that a monk commits murder or adultery as readily as he eats his dinner."[56] Imagination, of course, is open to various impressions. It is because "Catholicism appeals to the imagination, as a great fact, wherever she comes," that Protestantism has to impress upon the popular imagination that the Church is "Anti-Christ."[57] Such impressions "do not depend afterwards upon the facts or reasonings by which they were produced, any more than a blow, when once given, has any continued connection with the stone or the stick which gave it."[58] The anti-Catholic prejudice remains as a "stain on the mind."[59]

In his effort to show that the English imagination has been fatally poisoned at the wells, Newman deploys some of the most startling and vivid imagery to be found in his writings. He enjoys turning the images that have stained the Protestant imagination against Protestantism itself. Thus it is not a Catholic country but Protestant England which, "as far as religion is concerned, really must be called one large convent, or rather workhouse; the old pictures hang on the walls; the world-wide Church is chalked up on every side as a wivern or a griffin; no pure gleam of light finds its way in or from without; the thick atmosphere refracts and distorts such straggling rays as gain admittance."[60] The fact is, Newman argues, the "anti-Catholic Tradition" is the most effective weapon the Established Church has, and so its special duty is "to preserve it from rust and decay, to keep it bright and keen, and ready for action on any emergency or peril."[61] The Church of England's mission lies in "cataloguing and classing the texts which are to batter us, and the objections which are to explode

among us, and the insinuations and the slanders which are to
mow us down." The "Establishment is the Keeper in ordinary
of those national types and blocks from which Popery is ever
to be printed off."[62]

Some facts are useful for nurturing the tradition, and so it
is not surprising that "preachers and declaimers" have "now a
weary while been longing, and panting, and praying for some
good fat scandal, one, only just one . . . to batten upon and
revel in!"[63] The prejudiced Protestant is the child of the tradition, "and, like a man who has been for a long while in one
position, he is cramped and disabled, and has a difficulty and
pain . . . in stretching his limbs, straightening them, and moving them freely."[64] In his view the Catholic Church of England "ought to be content with vegetating, as a sickly plant,
in some back-yard or garret window";[65] for his part, he "is
intensely conscious that he is in a very eligible situation, and
his opponent in the gutter; and he lectures down upon him,
as if out of a drawing-room window."[66] Meanwhile,

> the meetings and preachings which are ever going on against us
> on all sides, though they may have no argumentative force what-
> ever, are still immense factories for the creation of prejudice,—
> an article, by means of these exertions, more carefully elabo-
> rated, and more lasting in its texture, than any specimens of
> hardware, or other material productions, which are the boast of
> a town such as this is.

Sometimes the imagery has a savage, Swiftian flavor, at
other times, as here, the effect is grotesque in the Dickens
manner. Or again, the imagery may be characteristically New-
manian in its sharply concrete psychological detail:

> If, for instance, a person cannot open a door, or get a key into
> a lock, which he has done a hundred times before, you know how
> apt he is to shake, and to rattle, and to force it, as if some great
> insult was offered him by its resistance: you know how surprised
> a wasp, or other large insect is, that he cannot get through a
> window-pane; such is the feeling of the Prejudiced man when

we urge our objections—not softened by them at all, but exasper-
ated the more. . . .[67]

Faced with the inescapable fact that people are converted
to Catholicism,

> the Prejudiced Man has a last resource, he simply forgets that
> Protestants they ever were . . . they merge in the great fog, in
> which to his eyes everything Catholic is enveloped: they are
> dwellers in the land of romance and fable; and, if he dimly
> contemplates them plunging and floundering amid the gloom, it
> is as griffins, wiverns, salamanders, the spawn of Popery, such
> as are said to sport in the depths of the sea, or to range amid the
> central sands of Africa.[68]

Catholic attempts to be conciliatory are doomed, for "our
advances are met as would be those of some hideous baboon,
or sloth, or rattlesnake, or toad, which strove to make itself
agreeable."[69] As for Catholic beliefs, they are as likely to "gain
admittance into his imagination, as for a lighted candle to
remain burning, when dipped into a vessel of water."[70] Catholic doctrines "stand in Reformation Tracts, torn up by the
roots or planted head-downwards," not "as they are found in
our own garden."[71] And they are too "great to be comfortably
accommodated in a Protestant nutshell."[72] For just as Protestantism has its Scripture "texts," so it has "its chips, shavings,
brick-bats, potsherds, and other odds and ends of the Heavenly City, which form the authenticated and ticketed specimens of what the Catholic Religion is in its great national
Museum."[73] Protestants prefer to "keep at a convenient distance from us, take the angles, calculate the sines and cosines,
and work out an algebraic process, when common sense would
bid them ask us a few questions."[74] It is because "Catholics are
to be surveyed from without, not inspected from within," that
"texts and formulas are to prevail over broad and luminous
facts" and "one grain of Protestant logic is to weigh more than
cartloads of Catholic testimony."[75] As for personal acquaintance, "Did the figures come down from some old piece of

tapestry, or were a lion rampant from an inn door suddenly to walk the streets, a Protestant would not be more surprised than at the notion that we have nerves, that we have hearts, that we have sensibilities."[76] "They will" even "do all in their power not to see you; the nearer you come, they will close their eyelids all the tighter; they will be very angry and frightened, and give the alarm as if you were going to murder them."[77]

The fact is that if "Catholicism were taken from the market," then "scandal" would be without "its staple food and its cheap luxuries," while prejudice "could not fast for a day," "would be in torment inexpressible, and call it Popish persecution, to be kept on this sort of meagre for a Lent, and would shake down Queen and Parliament with the violence of its convulsions, rather than it should never suck a Catholic's sweet bones and drink his blood any more."[78] Indeed, "Prejudice is ever craving for food, victuals are in constant request for its consumption every day; and accordingly they are served up in unceasing succession, Titus Oates, Maria Monk, and Jeffreys, being the purveyors, and platform and pulpit speakers being the cooks."[79]

As Newman warms to his theme, the humor becomes more and more fantastically grotesque, in the Dickensian vein. Protestantism, declares Newman, "is the current coin of the realm," so that "there is an incessant, unwearied circulation of Protestantism all over the country, for 365 days in the year from morning till night."[80] But converts present an unfamiliar phenomenon to the Protestant tradition, whose champions Newman advises to "be sure to shoot your game sitting; keep yourselves under cover," and from there, "Open your wide mouth, and collect your rumbling epithets, and round your pretentious sentences, and discharge your concentrated malignity."[81]

Nowhere else in his writings is Newman more exuberantly funny. Bully and monster as the Protestant tradition may be, it is also depicted as absurd and ridiculous. For example, Newman's own cellars at the Oratory have fallen under its suspicion. But the reason for the cellars is that the unevenness of the ground dictates some such construction under the building—and "there is a prejudice among Catholics in favour of horizontal floors."[82] No doubt, Newman muses, if the "nascent fable" had not "been lost by bad nursing," but had "been cherished awhile in those underground receptacles where first it drew breath," it might have lingered in the Protestant consciousness, and one day "a mob might have swarmed about our innocent dwelling, to rescue certain legs of mutton and pats of butter from imprisonment, and to hold an inquest over a dozen packing-cases, some old hampers, a knife-board, and a range of empty blacking bottles."[83] Instead, Newman has exposed the slander—although "it is a matter of surprise" that "we dare to speak a word in our defence, and that we are not content with the liberty of breathing, eating, moving about, and dying in a Protestant soil."[84] As for a Catholic priest, "there is peril in his frown, there is greater peril in his smile . . . whether he eats or sleeps, in every mouthful and every nod he ever has in view one and one only object, the aggrandisement of the unwearied, relentless foe of freedom and progress, the Catholic Church."[85] Prejudice, after all, "is superior to facts, and lives in a world of its own."[86]

Before leaving this minor masterpiece that has been neglected for far too long, it is worth noting one particularly brilliant touch of satire. For it is not just a question of attacking the religious complacency and provincialism of Victorian England which makes it possible for anyone to be "thought qualified to attack or to instruct a Catholic in matters of his religion; a country gentleman, a navy captain, a half-pay officer, with time on his hands, never having seen a Catholic, or a Catholic ceremonial, or a Catholic treatise, in his life, is competent, by means of one or two periodicals and tracts, and a set of Protestant extracts against Popery, to teach the Pope in his own religion, and refute a Council."[87] But rather the religious narrowness is only one, though a prominent, aspect of an aggressive, insular culture. The following passage, then, is pure Newman, but it is also a remarkable anticipation of

Dickens's satirical portrait of Mr. Podsnap in *Our Mutual Friend* (1865):

> They themselves are the pattern-men; their height, their dress, their manners, their food, their language, are all founded in the nature of things; and everything else is good or bad, just in that very degree in which it partakes, or does not partake, of them. All men ought to get up at half-past eight, breakfast between nine and ten, read the newspapers, lunch, take a ride or drive, dine. Here is the great principle of the day—dine; no one is a man who does not dine; yes, dine, and at the right hour; and it must *be* a dinner, with a certain time after dinner, and then, in due time, to bed. Tea and toast, port wine, roast beef; mincepies at Christmas, lamb at Easter, goose at Michaelmas, these are their great principles. They suspect any one who does otherwise. Figs and maccaroni for the day's fare, or Burgundy and grapes for breakfast!—they are aghast at the atrocity of the notion.[88]

III

Finally, something should be said about Newman's rhetoric, which, of course, it is impossible to consider apart from his thought. Consequently, such attention as has already been paid to his most characteristic mode of argument has revealed the pattern which informs his rhetorical art. Moreover, since Newman's own mind was marked by opposing tendencies, like, to take the most obvious example, his innate conservatism on the one hand and on the other a radical openness to new ideas, it is not perhaps surprising that his characteristic method of arguing is to keep in balance two extreme points of view in any argument. And his solution to problems tends not so much to be to find a compromise or middle way as to open up a way to a third, distinct position which does justice to the different truths in the opposed positions, that are then seen to be both partly yet not wholly true.

As has been said, sometimes the antithetical rhetoric simply sustains the tension between two opposite but valid views,
as in his tract "On the Introduction of Rationalistic Principles
into Revealed Religion." But at other times "thesis" and "antithesis" have to give way to a "synthesis" revealed by a change
of perspective. Such a method of arguing arose naturally out
of the attempt to construct a theology of the "Via Media."
But from a literary point of view, it is perhaps not until the
Idea of a University that the argument and the rhetoric fully
become one. Our discussion of the ecclesiology of the last
chapter of the *Apologia* has already highlighted the dramatic
and subtle rhetoric with which Newman forges an approach
to the relationship between authority and freedom in the
Church that transcends both the rival positions. In the *Idea*
the denouement is, if anything, even more dramatically surprising, although there is not quite the same sharply poised
balance held between two rival positions as in the *Apologia*.

At the heart of the rhetoric of the *Discourses* is the tension
between the genuinely unconditional insistence on the absolute value of knowledge in itself and the equally firm conviction that knowledge is emphatically not the highest good.[89]
Thus, while on the one hand Newman will have no party with
those who wish to justify education solely on moral or religious
grounds, on the other hand, without any self-contradiction,
he insists that it is better to have a simple religious faith than
an educated intellect without religious belief. There is no
question of any necessary incompatibility for Newman, but
he recognizes the fact that religion and education, faith and
reason, are not always found together: "Right Reason, that is,
Reason rightly exercised, leads the mind to the Catholic
Faith, and plants it there, and teaches it in all its religious
speculations to act under its guidance. But Reason, considered
as a real agent in the world, and as an operative principle in
man's nature . . . is far from taking so straight and satisfactory
a direction."[90] If, then, there has to be a choice between this
kind of reason and simple faith, Newman leaves us in no

doubt as to his own preference. These are the two distinct priorities which Newman contrives to balance in sharp equipoise through the *Discourses*.

The point can be illustrated first by some simple examples. For instance, the various eulogies of man's "imperial intellect"[91] receive their counterpoint, as it were, in the eloquent expositions of the omnipotence and omniscience of God and the authority of the Catholic Church and the papacy. Or there is the contrast in the final Discourse between the admission that a Christian literature is an impossibility, because it "is a contradiction in terms to attempt a sinless Literature of sinful man," and the insistence that nevertheless the study of literature must not be omitted from education, because education is "for this world" and "it is not the way to learn to swim in troubled waters, never to have gone into them."[92] Conversely, the rapt evocation of the wonder of music in the fourth Discourse is promptly followed by a warning against its temptation "rather to use Religion than to minister to it."[93]

In general, the eulogy of a liberal education is systematically qualified by reminders of its limitations. Thus the definition of a "liberal" pursuit does not attempt to pretend that "in point of worth and importance" there need be even any comparison with an "illiberal" study: "even what is supernatural need not be liberal, nor need a hero be a gentleman, for the plain reason that one idea is not another idea."[94] Newman is keenly aware of the danger of exaggerating the importance both of the university and of a liberal education. It is, he insists, "as real a mistake to burden" liberal knowledge "with virtue or religion as with the mechanical arts":

> Its direct business is not to steel the soul against temptation or to console it in affliction, any more than to set the loom in motion, or to direct the steam carriage . . . it as little mends our hearts as it improves our temporal circumstances. . . . Quarry the granite rock with razors, or moor the vessel with a thread of silk; then you may hope with such keen and delicate instruments as

human knowledge and human reason to contend against those giants, the passion and the pride of man.[95]

Again, the "perfection of the Intellect, which is the result of Education" may have "almost the beauty and harmony of heavenly contemplation, so intimate is it with the eternal order of things and the music of the spheres"—but, Newman emphasizes, it is not to be confused with the "vast ideas or dazzling projects" of genius.[96] In practice, too, "a so-called University, which dispensed with residence and tutorial superintendence, and gave its degrees to any person who passed an examination in a wide range of subjects," may even be "*morally* the better" than "a University which had no professors or examinations at all, but merely brought a number of young men together for three or four years"—but "if I must determine which of the two courses was the more successful in training, moulding, enlarging the mind . . . I have no hesitation in giving the preference to that University which did nothing": such a university, with "a heathen code of ethics," at least "can boast of a succession of heroes and statesmen, of literary men and philosophers, of men conspicuous for great natural virtues, for habits of business, for knowledge of life, for practical judgment, for cultivated tastes, for accomplishments, who have made England what it is,—able to subdue the earth, able to domineer over Catholics."[97]

An element of suspense hangs more or less continuously over the *Discourses* as evaluations are constantly modified by the author's changing point of view. Thus the Discourse from which we have just quoted ends with a description of "the poor boy" in Crabbe's poem who managed "to fashion for himself a philosophy" from his humble country experiences— "how much more genuine an education," Newman exclaims, than that of those university students "who are forced to load their minds with a score of subjects against an examination!"[98]

But the most remarkable and dramatic shift of perspective in the *Discourses* is to be found in its most famous part—the celebrated protrait of the "gentleman" in the eighth Discourse. It is here that Newman concludes his exposition of intellectual culture with an eloquent depiction of its "momentous" moral influences "all upon the type of Christianity . . . so much so, that a character more noble to look at, more beautiful, more winning, in the various relations of life and in personal duties, is hardly conceivable." However, "the work is as certainly not supernatural as it is certainly noble and beautiful," for there is a "radical difference" between this "mental refinement" and "genuine religion."[99] And Newman proceeds to show how "the tendency of the intellectual culture" is to become "a false philosophy" and a "spurious religion."[100] He takes as an example the Emperor Julian, "in whom every Catholic sees the shadow of the future Antichrist," but who "was all but the pattern-man of philosophical virtue."[101] Indeed, it is from the very "shallowness of philosophical Religion . . . that its disciples seem able to fulfil certain precepts of Christianity more readily and exactly than Christians themselves," so that "the school of the world seems to send out living copies" of "St. Paul's exemplar of the Christian in his external relations . . . with greater success than the Church."[102] Modesty is substituted for humility, and "pride, under such training, instead of running to waste in the education of the mind, is turned to account." A passage of marvelous irony follows, in which Newman admiringly extols the great and real social fruits of this new quality "called self-respect," only to conclude with devastating effect: "It breathes upon the face of the community, and the hollow sepulchre is forthwith beautiful to look upon." Still, however, we are not allowed to forget that secular education can accomplish objects which seem to defeat religion, and we are reminded that it is a refined self-respect which "is now quietly but energetically opposing itself to the unchristian practice of duelling . . . and certainly it seems likely to effect what Religion has aimed at abolishing in vain."[103]

The famous passage which follows, beginning with the well-known words, "Hence it is that it is almost a definition

of a gentleman to say he is one who never inflicts pain,"[104] is
so eloquent and presents such an attractive picture that many
people have supposed that this is in fact Newman's ideal. And
indeed they are right in the sense that it is the ideal end of a
liberal education, which

> makes not the Christian, not the Catholic, but the gentleman.
> It is well to be a gentleman, it is well to have a cultivated
> intellect, a delicate taste, a candid, equitable, dispassionate
> mind, a noble and courteous bearing in the conduct of life;—
> these are the connatural qualities of a large knowledge; they are
> the objects of a University; I am advocating, I shall illustrate and
> insist upon them; but still, I repeat, they are no guarantee for
> sanctity or even for conscientiousness, they may attach to the
> man of the world, to the profligate, to the heartless. . . .[105]

The last terse sentence of Discourse VIII makes the point
concretely and also dramatically: "Basil and Julian were fel-
low-students at the schools of Athens; and one became the
Saint and Doctor of the Church, the other her scoffing and
relentless foe."[106] It is a striking conclusion to one of the
greatest passages of rhetoric in the English language.

ABBREVIATIONS

NEWMAN COLLECTED HIS WORKS in a uniform edition of 36 vols. (1868–81). Until his death in 1890 he continued making minor textual changes in reprints of individual volumes in this edition, of which all the volumes from 1886 were published by Longmans, Green, and Co. of London. References are usually to volumes in the uniform edition published after 1890 by Longmans, which are distinguished from other editions by not including publication details in brackets after the title.

Apo.	*Apologia pro Vita Sua,* ed. Martin J. Svaglic (Oxford: Clarendon Press, 1967)
Ari.	*The Arians of the Fourth Century*
AW	*John Henry Newman: Autobiographical Writings,* ed. Henry Tristram (London and New York: Sheed and Ward, 1956)
Call.	*Callista: A Tale of the Third Century*
Cons.	*On Consulting the Faithful in Matters of Doctrine,* ed. John Coulson (London: Geoffrey Chapman, 1961)
DA	*Discussions and Arguments on Various Subjects*
Dev.	*An Essay on the Development of Christian Doctrine,* 6th ed., Foreword by Ian Ker (Notre Dame, Ind.: University of Notre Dame Press, 1989)

Diff. i, ii	*Certain Difficulties felt by Anglicans in Catholic Teaching,* 2 vols.
Ess. i, ii	*Essays Critical and Historical,* 2 vols.
GA	*An Essay in Aid of a Grammar of Assent,* ed. I. T. Ker (Oxford: Clarendon Press, 1985)
HS i, ii, iii	*Historical Sketches,* 3 vols.
Idea	*The Idea of a University,* ed. I. T. Ker (Oxford: Clarendon Press, 1976)
Jfc.	*Lectures on the Doctrine of Justification*
LD	*The Letters and Diaries of John Henry Newman,* ed. Charles Stephen Dessain et al., vols. i–vi (Oxford: Clarendon Press, 1978–84), xi–xxii (London: Nelson, 1961–72), xxiii–xxxi (Oxford: Clarendon Press, 1973–77)
LG	*Loss and Gain: The Story of a Convert*
Mix.	*Discourses addressed to Mixed Congregations*
OS	*Sermons preached on Various Occasions*
PS i-viii	*Parochial and Plain Sermons,* 8 vols.
Phil.N. i, ii	*The Philosophical Notebook of John Henry Newman,* ed. Edward Sillem, 2 vols. (Louvain: Nauwelaerts, 1969–70)
Prepos.	*Present Position of Catholics in England*
TP i	*The Theological Papers of John Henry Newman on Faith and Certainty,* ed. Hugo M. de Achaval, S.J., and J. Derek Holmes (Oxford: Clarendon Press, 1976)
TP ii	*The Theological Papers of John Henry Newman on Biblical Inspiration and on Infallibility,* ed. J. Derek Holmes (Oxford: Clarendon Press, 1979)
US	*Fifteen Sermons preached before the University of Oxford*
VM i, ii	*The Via Media,* 2 vols.

NOTES

1. THE EDUCATOR

1. See *Idea*, pp. xxix–xxxi.
2. *LD* xv. 226.
3. See below, chap. 5.
4. *LD* xxiv. 390.
5. *AW* 259.
6. *AW* 49.
7. *AW* 63.
8. *LD* xxii. 218.
9. *LD* xiv. 213.
10. *LD* xxvi. 58.
11. *LD* xix. 464.
12. *LD* xxi. 51.
13. *LD* xxiii. 117.
14. *Idea* 96–97.
15. Martin J. Svaglic, ed., *The Idea of a University* (Notre Dame, Ind.: University of Notre Dame Press, 1982), p. xxi.
16. A. Dwight Culler, *The Imperial Intellect: A Study of Newman's Educational Ideal* (New Haven, Conn., and London: Yale University Press, 1955), 182.
17. See Culler, *The Imperial Intellect*, 185–86, 200–203, 371.
18. *Idea* 10–11.
19. *Idea* 114.
20. *Idea* 103–4.
21. Culler, *The Imperial Intellect*, 203.
22. *Idea* 193–94, 197, 245.
23. *Idea* 216, 221–22.

24. *Idea* 10–11.

25. *Idea* 12–13.

26. *Idea* 57.

27. *Idea* 111.

28. *Idea* 113.

29. Raymond Williams, *Culture and Society 1780–1950* (New York: Columbia University Press, 1958), 110–11.

30. *Idea* 144–45.

31. Matthew Arnold, *Culture and Anarchy with Friendship's Garland and Some Literary Essays,* ed. R. H. Super (Ann Arbor: University of Michigan Press, 1965), 233.

32. *Idea* 114.

33. *Idea* 116–17.

34. *Idea* 120–21.

35. *Idea* 122–23.

36. *Idea* 123–24.

37. *Idea* 125–28.

38. *HS* iii. 13.

39. So important does Newman regard "the personal presence of a teacher"—the "great instrument, or rather organ" of a university—that in his collected volume of essays *Office and Work of Universities* (1856) he says that "An academical system without the personal influence of teachers upon pupils, is an arctic winter; it will create an ice-bound, petrified, cast-iron University, and nothing else." And he continues, in a well-known autobiographical passage about his own undergraduate experience at Oxford:

> I have experienced a state of things, in which teachers were cut off from the taught as by an insurmountable barrier; when neither party entered into the thoughts of the other; when each lived by and in itself; when the tutor was supposed to fulfil his duty, if he trotted on like a squirrel in his cage, if at a certain hour he was in a certain room, or in hall, or in chapel, as it might be; and the pupil did his duty too, if he was careful to meet his tutor in that same room, or hall, or chapel, at the same certain hour; and when neither the one nor the other dreamed of seeing each other out of lecture, out of chapel, out of academical gown. I have known places where a stiff manner, a pompous voice, coldness and condescension, were the teacher's attributes . . . (*HS* iii. 14, 74–75).

40. *Idea* 129–32.
41. *Idea* 134–35, 145–46, 154.
42. *Idea* 272–75.
43. *Idea* 10–11.
44. *Idea* 341.
45. *Idea* 393–94.
46. *Idea* 302.
47. *Idea* 394, 398, 401, 403–4.
48. *Idea* 5.
49. *Idea* 33.
50. *Idea* 57.
51. *Idea* 183.
52. *Idea* 38.
53. *Idea* 52.
54. *Idea* 57.
55. *Idea* 64.
56. *Idea* 54–57.
57. *Idea* 73–74.
58. *Idea* 76.
59. *Idea* 81.
60. *Idea* 84, 86, 87.
61. *Idea* 73.
62. *Idea* 407.
63. *Idea* 145–46.
64. *Idea* 94–96.
65. *Idea* 185.
66. *Idea* 369–72.

2. THE PHILOSOPHER

1. *LD* i. 219, 225–26.
2. GA 109.
3. DA 295.
4. The following summary is an adapted version of the summary in my *John Henry Newman: A Biography* (Oxford: Clarendon Press, 1988), chap. 6.
5. US 177, 179, 182–84, 187–88, 190–93, 197–201.
6. *Idea* 371.
7. US 203–4, 207, 209, 211–13, 215, 218.

8. US 224–28, 230, 232–34, 236, 239, 249–50.
9. US 253–60, 262, 266–67, 271–72, 274, 276.
10. US 279, 287, 289–92.
11. LD xxiv. 275–76.
12. LD xi. 293; xv. 381.
13. Apo. 31.
14. Dev. 107, 123, 115, 327.
15. LD xi. 289.
16. LD xv. 457–58.
17. LD xix. 460.
18. LD xxi. 146.
19. LD xxiv. 146.
20. Mix. 234.
21. LD xiii. 267.
22. TP i. 11, 31–32.
23. TP i. 121–22.
24. TP i. 122–27.
25. Phil. N. ii. 29, 35, 73, 75, 130.
26. US 18.
27. Phil. N. ii. 31.
28. Call. 314.
29. Apo. 180.
30. LD xix. 294.
31. LD xxv. 35.
32. AW 270.
33. LD xxv. 35, 29, 199.
34. See GA pp. xliii–xliv.
35. The following summary of the argument and part of the ensuing discussion are taken from my John Henry Newman: A Biography, chap. 16, with some modifications.
36. GA 20.
37. GA 13–14.
38. GA 18.
39. GA 20.
40. GA 22–25.
41. GA 27.
42. GA 30.
43. GA 33–34.
44. GA 55.

45. GA 58.
46. GA 72–76, 79, 82–83, 88.
47. GA 31.
48. GA 14.
49. GA 13.
50. GA 24–25.
51. GA 36, 42.
52. GA 45, 48–49, 55–56, 58, 62–63.
53. GA 251.
54. GA 106.
55. GA 112.
56. GA 116.
57. GA 120.
58. GA 124.
59. GA 128.
60. GA 145.
61. GA 152.
62. GA 185.
63. GA 196.
64. GA 205–6.
65. GA 207–8.
66. GA 221.
67. GA 222–23.
68. GA 224.
69. GA 226.
70. GA 231.
71. GA 264.
72. GA 266.
73. GA 250.
74. GA 9–10.
75. GA 112.
76. GA 114.
77. GA 116.
78. GA 105.
79. GA 221.
80. GA 228.
81. GA 231.
82. GA 228, 205–6.
83. GA 190.

84. GA 205.
85. GA 214.
86. GA 145.
87. GA 150–51.
88. GA 153.
89. GA 167.
90. GA 165.
91. GA 166.
92. See GA 348–49.
93. Cf. J. M. Cameron, "Newman and Locke: A Note on Some Themes in *An Essay in Aid of a Grammar of Assent*," *Newman Studien*, vol. 9 (Nuremberg: Glock and Lutz, 1974), pp. 204–5.
94. GA 224.
95. *Phil. N.* ii. 30.
96. Frederick Copleston, S.J., *A History of Philosophy*, vol. 8 (Westminster, Md.: The Newman Press, 1966), p. 516 n. 2.

3. THE PREACHER

1. See R. D. Middleton, "The Vicar of St. Mary's," in *John Henry Newman: Centenary Essays* (Westminster, Md.: Newman Bookshop, 1945), 127–38; David J. DeLaura, "'O Unforgotten Voice': The Memory of Newman in the Nineteenth Century," in *Sources for Reinterpretation: The Use of Nineteenth-century Literary Documents. Essays in Honor of C. L. Cline* (Austin: University of Texas Press, 1975), 23–55.
2. The following discussion of the realism of the sermons is an adapted and modified version of part of the critique of the *Parochial and Plain Sermons* in my *John Henry Newman: A Biography*, chap. 2.
3. *PS* i. 13, 82.
4. *PS* viii. 242–23.
5. *PS* i. 67, 69.
6. *PS* i. 252.
7. *PS* i. 114.
8. *PS* ii. 159.
9. *LD* xi. 191; xiv. 153.
10. *PS* iii. 211.
11. *PS* i. 11.

12. *PS* i. 69.
13. *PS* i. 68.
14. *PS* i. 95.
15. *PS* iii. 238; iv. 5; v. 241, 244–45.
16. *PS* i. 41–43.
17. *PS* i. 51.
18. *PS* i. 27–28, 35, 172.
19. *PS* i. 17, 54, 81; ii. 29, 179; v. 31; vi. 95, 263–64, 266.
20. *PS* v. 33, 39, 36, 43.
21. *PS* viii. 265.
22. *PS* v. 42
23. *PS* ii. 371.
24. *PS* i. 70.
25. *PS* i. 233.
26. *PS* i. 270.
27. *PS* ii. 55.
28. *PS* ii. 367.
29. *PS* i. 61–62.
30. *PS* iv. 14, 153.
31. *PS* v. 256.
32. *PS* i. 84.
33. *PS* ii. 389, 199.
34. *PS* vi. 80.
35. *PS* iv. 154–57.
36. *PS* iv. 301; vii. 180.
37. *PS* iii. 30; vii. 22.
38. *LD* v. 327.
39. *PS* iii. 130–31.
40. *PS* ii. 167.
41. *PS* vi. 45.
42. *PS* vi. 73, 76.
43. James Anthony Froude, *Short Studies on Great Subjects,* fourth series (New York: Charles Scribner's Sons, 1910), 188.
44. *PS* ii. 222.
45. *PS* iii. 267–68.
46. *PS* ii. 35.
47. *LD* v. 14–15, 22.
48. *PS* i. 23–24.
49. *PS* ii. 286, 282.

50. *PS* iv. 324.
51. *PS* iv. 337–38.
52. *PS* v. 66.
53. *PS* v. 271.
54. *PS* vi. 121.
55. *PS* v. 48.
56. *PS* vii. 12.
57. Froude, *Short Studies on Great Subjects*, 186.
58. *PS* i. 136.
59. *PS* i. 25.
60. *PS* i. 169.
61. *PS* i. 46–47.
62. *PS* i. 71.
63. *PS* i. 169–70.
64. *PS* ii. 75–76, 272–73.
65. *PS* iv. 42–43.
66. *PS* i. 90.
67. *PS* i. 73.
68. *PS* i. 131.
69. *PS* iii. 13.
70. *PS* iv. 33.
71. *PS* iv. 15.
72. *PS* i. 110.
73. *PS* i. 90.
74. *PS* i. 114.
75. *PS* i. 167–68.
76. *PS* v. 108.
77. *PS* i. 102.
78. *PS* iv. 42.
79. *PS* i. 142.
80. *PS* iv. 72.
81. *PS* iii. 67.
82. *PS* iii. 295.
83. *PS* iv. 95.
84. *PS* iv. 44, 45, 47.
85. *PS* v. 143, 232.
86. *PS* v. 350.
87. *PS* viii. 71.
88. *PS* v. 212–13, 217.

4. THE THEOLOGIAN

1. *Ari.* 147–48, 274.
2. *Apo.* 37.
3. *Ari.* 36–37, 145–46.
4. *Apo.* 36.
5. *Ari.* 82, 84.
6. *Ess.* i. 31–32, 41.
7. *DA* 18–19, 2.
8. *VM* i. 15–18.
9. *DA* 295.
10. *VM* i. 19, 129, 23–24.
11. Unpublished letter to Mrs. W. Froude, 9 Dec. 1843 (Birmingham Oratory Archives).
12. *VM* i. 26–27, 245, 250–52, 286.
13. *Jfc.*, p.v.
14. *Jfc.* 2.
15. *Jfc.* 30–31, 34.
16. *Jfc.* 56.
17. *Jfc.* 263–66.
18. *Jfc.* 15.
19. *Jfc.* 72–73.
20. *Jfc.* 78.
21. *Jfc.* 81.
22. *Jfc.* 96, 99, 174.
23. *Jfc.* 136–38.
24. *Jfc.* 154.
25. *Dev.* 29–30, 5.
26. *Dev.* 38.
27. *Dev.* 34–36, 38–40.
28. *Dev.* 171.
29. *Dev.* 97–98.
30. *Dev.* 100.
31. *Dev.* 321–22.
32. *Apo.* 108.
33. *Apo.* 110–12.
34. *Diff.* i. 379.
35. Jaroslav Pelikan, *Development of Christian Doctrine: Some Historical Prolegomena* (New Haven and London: Yale University Press, 1969), 3.

36. Owen Chadwick, *From Bossuet to Newman: The Idea of Doctrinal Development* (Cambridge: Cambridge University Press, 1957), 157–60, 195. For this and similar criticisms, see Ian T. Ker, "Newman's Theory—Development or Continuing Revelation?" *Newman and Gladstone Centennial Essays*, ed. James D. Bastable (Dublin: Veritas Publications, 1978), 145–59.

37. US 321.

38. *Dev.* 191–92.

39. *Dev.* 52–53.

40. TP ii. 156–59.

41. LD xix. 135.

42. LD xix. 141.

43. *Cons.* 54–55.

44. *Cons.* 63.

45. *Cons.* 72.

46. *Cons.* 75–76, 77, 106.

47. The discussions that follow of the *Apologia, Letter to Pusey, Letter to the Duke of Norfolk,* and the Preface to the *Via Media* contain material which I have adapted, recast, and revised from my treatment of these writings in my *John Henry Newman: A Biography*.

48. *Apo.* 220, 224–25.

49. *Apo.* 225–26.

50. *Apo.* 226, 229–31.

51. *Apo.* 231–33.

52. *Apo.* 237–38.

53. *Apo.* 238–41.

54. *Diff.* ii. 12.

55. *Diff.* ii. 18–21.

56. *Diff.* ii. 26.

57. *Diff.* ii. 28.

58. LD xxii. 149.

59. *Diff.* ii. 78–79.

60. *Diff.* ii. 80.

61. *Diff.* ii. 81.

62. LD xx. 470–71.

63. *Diff.* ii. 89.

64. LD xxvii. 139.

65. LD xx. 465.

66. *Diff.* ii. 92–93.

67. *Diff.* ii. 99–100.

68. *Diff.* ii. 106–7.
69. *Diff.* ii. 105.
70. *Diff.* ii. 115–16.
71. *Ess.* ii. 101.
72. *Diff.* ii. 372.
73. *LD* xxv. 71.
74. *Diff.* ii. 335.
75. *Diff.* ii. 337.
76. *Diff.* ii. 330.
77. *LD* xxv. 284.
78. *LD* xxv. 447.
79. *LD* xxvi. 35.
80. *LD* xxvii. 338.
81. *Diff.* ii. 280.
82. *Diff.* ii. 332.
83. *Diff.* ii. 320–21.
84. *Diff.* ii. 334.
85. *Diff.* ii. 307.
86. *Diff.* ii. 247–50.
87. *Diff.* ii. 252–54.
88. *Diff.* ii. 256–58.
89. *Diff.* ii. 261.
90. *LD* xxvii. 70.
91. *VM* i, pp. xxxvi–xxxvii.
92. *VM* i, pp. xxxviii–xliii.
93. *VM* i, pp. xlvii–xlviii.
94. *VM* i, pp. xlviii–l, lii–lvi.
95. *LD* xxv. 31–32; xxii. 99.
96. *VM* i, pp. lxvi–lxxi, lxxiv–lxxvi.
97. *VM* i, pp. lxxx–lxxxi, lxxxvi.
98. *VM* i, p. xciv.
99. C. Stephen Dessain, "Newman's Spirituality: Its Value Today," *English Spiritual Writers*, ed. Charles Davis (New York: Sheed and Ward, 1962), 160.

5. THE WRITER

1. *HS* i. 297.
2. *LD* xxiv. 242.

3. F. W. Newman, *Contributions chiefly to the early History of the late Cardinal Newman*, 2nd ed. (London: Kegan Paul, 1891), 44.

4. *HS* i. 293–94.

5. J. M. Cameron, *John Henry Newman* (London: 1956), 7.

6. *LD* iv. 106.

7. *LD* xxi. 167.

8. *LD* xx. 494.

9. *LD* vi. 352.

10. *LD* xx. 208–9.

11. *LD* xx. 216.

12. *LD* xxi. 13–14.

13. *Apo.* 352.

14. *Apo.* 388–89.

15. *Apo.* 415.

16. *LD* iii. 257–58.

17. *LD* iii. 298.

18. *LD* i. 364.

19. *LD* vi. 13.

20. *Ess.* i. 152.

21. *Ess.* i. 311–12.

22. *Ess.* ii. 138–39, 134.

23. *HS* i. 420–21.

24. *Ess.* ii. 340–41.

25. The following discussions of the *Tamworth Reading Room, Loss and Gain, Difficulties of Anglicans,* and *Present Position of Catholics,* contain material, which I have adapted, recast, and revised, from my *John Henry Newman: A Biography.*

26. DA 261–62, 264, 266–68.

27. DA 269–70, 272.

28. DA 277, 281–82.

29. DA 279–82.

30. LG 74, 84–85.

31. LG 351.

32. *LD* xv. 399; xiv. 360.

33. LG 80.

34. *Mix.* 105, 200.

35. OS 147–48, 156–57.

36. OS 148–51.

37. *Diff.* i. 16.

38. *Diff.* i. 4.

39. *Diff.* i. 25.
40. *Diff.* i. 35.
41. *Diff.* i. 150.
42. *Diff.* i. 15.
43. *Diff.* i. 178.
44. *Diff.* i. 289–90.
45. *Diff.* i. 10, 12.
46. *Diff.* i. 152.
47. *Diff.* i. 106.
48. *Diff.* i. 162.
49. *Diff.* i. 167.
50. *Diff.* i. 169.
51. *Diff.* i. 193.
52. *Diff.* i. 235.
53. *LD* xxvi. 115.
54. For a fuller account of the book, see my *John Henry Newman: A Biography*, chap. 8.
55. *Prepos.* 2.
56. *Prepos.* 95.
57. *Prepos.* 224.
58. *Prepos.* 231.
59. *Prepos.* 233.
60. *Prepos.* 44.
61. *Prepos.* 74.
62. *Prepos.* 75.
63. *Prepos.* 139.
64. *Prepos.* 178.
65. *Prepos.* 195.
66. *Prepos.* 200.
67. *Prepos.* 240.
68. *Prepos.* 245.
69. *Prepos.* 265.
70. *Prepos.* 303.
71. *Prepos.* 331.
72. *Prepos.* 332.
73. *Prepos.* 342.
74. *Prepos.* 350.
75. *Prepos.* 358–59.
76. *Prepos.* 355.
77. *Prepos.* 372.

78. *Prepos.* 341.
79. *Prepos.* 371.
80. *Prepos.* 366.
81. *Prepos.* 376.
82. *Prepos.* 119.
83. *Prepos.* 124–25.
84. *Prepos.* 199.
85. *Prepos.* 248–49.
86. *Prepos.* 261.
87. *Prepos.* 330.
88. *Prepos.* 296.
89. The following discussion is based on part of my introduction to *Idea.*
90. *Idea* 157.
91. *Idea* 371.
92. *Idea* 195, 197.
93. *Idea* 80.
94. *Idea* 101.
95. *Idea* 110–11.
96. *Idea* 124.
97. *Idea* 129–30.
98. *Idea* 132–33.
99. *Idea* 164.
100. *Idea* 165.
101. *Idea* 167.
102. *Idea* 174.
103. *Idea* 177–78.
104. *Idea* 179.
105. *Idea* 110.
106. *Idea* 181.

SELECT BIBLIOGRAPHY

Texts

Uniform edition of works, 36 vols. (London, 1868–81).

Apologia pro Vita Sua, ed. Martin J. Svaglic (Oxford, 1967). Critical edition.

Autobiographical Writings, ed. Henry Tristram (London and New York, 1956).

Catholic Sermons of Cardinal Newman, ed. at the Birmingham Oratory (London, 1957).

An Essay in Aid of a Grammar of Assent, ed. I. T. Ker (Oxford, 1985). Critical edition.

The Idea of a University, ed. I. T. Ker (Oxford, 1976). Critical edition.

The Letters and Diaries of John Henry Newman, ed. Charles Stephen Dessain et al., vols. xi-xxii (London, 1961–72), xxiii-xxxi (Oxford, 1973–7), i-vi (Oxford, 1978–84).

Meditations and Devotions of the late Cardinal Newman (London, 1893).

My Campaign in Ireland, Part I, ed. W. Neville (privately printed, 1896).

Newman the Oratorian: His Unpublished Oratory Papers, ed. Placid Murray, O.S.B. (Dublin, 1969).

On Consulting the Faithful in Matters of Doctrine, ed. John Coulson (London, 1961).

On the Inspiration of Scripture: John Henry Newman, ed. J. Derek Holmes and Robert Murray, S.J. (London, 1967).

The Philosophical Notebook of John Henry Newman, ed. Edward Sillem, 2 vols. (Louvain, 1969–70).

Sermon Notes of John Henry Cardinal Newman, 1849–1878, ed. Fathers of the Birmingham Oratory (London, 1913).

The Theological Papers of John Henry Newman on Biblical Inspiration and on Infallibility, ed. J. Derek Holmes (Oxford, 1979).

The Theological Papers of John Henry Newman on Faith and Certainty, ed. Hugo M. de Achaval, S.J. and J. Derek Holmes (Oxford, 1976).

Biographical

Wilfrid Ward, *The Life of John Henry Cardinal Newman*, 2 vols. (London, 1912).

Meriol Trevor, *Newman: The Pillar of the Cloud; Newman: Light in Winter* (London, 1962). Abridged as *Newman's Journey* (Glasgow, 1974).

Ian Ker, *John Henry Newman: A Biography* (Oxford, 1988). An intellectual and literary life.

General

Richard H. Hutton, *Cardinal Newman* (2nd edn., London, 1891).

Wilfrid Ward, *Last Lectures* (London, 1918).

Charles Frederick Harrold, *John Henry Newman: An Expository and Critical Study of his Mind, Thought and Art* (London, 1945).

J. M. Cameron, *John Henry Newman* (London, 1956).

———, "John Henry Newman and the Tractarian Movement" in *Nineteenth Century Religious Thought in the West*, vol. 2, ed. Ninian Smart, John Clayton, Steven T. Katz, and Patrick Sherry (Cambridge, 1985).

Charles Stephen Dessain, *John Henry Newman* (London, 1966). The best introduction to and summary of his thought.

John Coulson and A. M. Allchin, eds., *The Rediscovery of Newman: An Oxford Symposium* (London, 1967).

Thomas Vargish, *Newman: The Contemplation of Mind* (Oxford, 1970).

Hilary Jenkins, "Religion and Secularism: The Contemporary Significance of Newman's Thought" in *Modes of Thought: Essays on*

Thinking in Western and Non-Western Societies, ed. Robin Horton and Ruth Finnegan (London, 1973).

The Educator

Fergal McGrath, S.J., *Newman's University: Idea and Reality* (London, 1951).

A. Dwight Culler, *The Imperial Intellect: A Study of Newman's Educational Ideal* (New Haven and London, 1955).

Martin J. Svaglic, ed., *The Idea of a University* (New York, 1960; Notre Dame, Ind., 1982).

I. T. Ker, ed., *The Idea of a University* (Oxford, 1976).

The Philosopher

John Hick, *Faith and Knowledge* (2nd edn., London, 1967), chap. 4.

H. H. Price, *Belief* (London, 1969), lectures 5, 6.

Edward Sillem, *The Philosophical Notebook of John Henry Newman* (Louvain, 1969), vol. 1, "General Introduction to the Study of Newman's Philosophy."

Nicholas Lash, ed., *An Essay in Aid of a Grammar of Assent* (Notre Dame and London, 1979).

M. Jamie Ferreira, *Doubt and Religious Commitment: The Role of the Will in Newman's Thought* (Oxford, 1980).

I. T. Ker, ed., *An Essay in Aid of a Grammar of Assent* (Oxford, 1985).

The Preacher

E. D. Mackerness, *The Heeded Voice: Studies in the Literary Status of the Anglican Sermon, 1830–1900* (Cambridge, 1959), chap. 1.

C. Stephen Dessain, "Newman's Spirituality: Its Value To-day" in *English Spiritual Writers,* ed. Charles Davis (London, 1961).

Hilda Graef, *God and Myself: The Spirituality of John Henry Newman* (London, 1967).

W. D. White, ed., *The Preaching of John Henry Newman* (Philadelphia, 1969).

The Theologian

Owen Chadwick, *From Bossuet to Newman: The Idea of Doctrinal Development* (Cambridge, 1957).

J. H. Walgrave, O.P., *Newman the Theologian: The Nature of Belief and Doctrine as exemplified in his Life and Works*, trans. A. V. Littledale (London, 1960).

————, *Unfolding Revelation: The Nature of Doctrinal Development* (Philadelphia, 1972), chap. 9.

Nicholas Lash, *Change in Focus: A Study of Doctrinal Change and Continuity* (London, 1973), chaps. 9, 10.

————, *Newman on Development: The Search for an Explanation in History* (London, 1975).

Robin C. Selby, *The Principle of Reserve in the Writings of John Henry Cardinal Newman* (Oxford, 1975).

Edward Jeremy Miller, *John Henry Newman on the Idea of Church* (Shepherdstown, W. Va., 1987).

The Writer

Walter E. Houghton, *The Art of Newman's Apologia* (New Haven, 1945).

John Holloway, *The Victorian Sage: Studies in Argument* (London, 1953), chap. 6.

John Beer, "Newman and the Romantic Sensibility" in *The English Mind: Studies in the English Moralists Presented to Basil Willey*, ed. Hugh Sykes Davies and George Watson (Cambridge, 1964).

Vincent Ferrer Blehl, S.J., and Francis X. Connolly, eds., *Newman's Apologia: A Classic Reconsidered* (New York, 1964).

Geoffrey Tillotson, "Newman the Writer" in Geoffrey and Kathleen Tillotson, *Mid-Victorian Studies* (London, 1965).

Linda H. Peterson, *Victorian Autobiography: The Tradition of Self-Interpretation* (New Haven and London, 1986), chap. 4.

INDEX

205